Human Rights,
Trade and Diplomacy
in Greek-German Relations,
1967–1974

Chrysa Vachtsevanou, Stefan Zeppenfeld,
Vangelis Karamanolakis (Eds.)

Human Rights, Trade and Diplomacy in Greek-German Relations, 1967–1974

Published on behalf of *Contemporary Social History Archives* (ASKI), Athens and *Archiv der sozialen Demokratie* (*AdsD*), Bonn.

Bibliographical information of the German National Library

The German National Library catalogues this publication in the German National Bibliography; detailed bibliographic information can be found on the internet at: http://dnb.dnb.de.

ISBN 978-3-8012-4256-5

Copyright © 2022 by
Verlag J.H.W. Dietz Nachf. GmbH
Dreizehnmorgenweg 24, D-53175 Bonn, Germany

Cover design: Jens Vogelsang, Aachen
Cover picture: © ASKI
Typesetting: Ralf Schnarrenberger, Hamburg
Printing and processing: Bookpress, Olsztyn

All rights reserved
Printed in Poland 2022

Find us on the internet: www.dietz-verlag.de

9
Preface

11
Chrysa Vachtsevanou, Vangelis Karamanolakis
Introduction

21
Chrysa Vachtsevanou
The Cradle of Democracy "in a Plaster Cast":
West German Foreign Policy towards
the Greek Military Dictatorship (1967–1974)

41
Dimitrios K. Apostolopoulos
The German Federal Government
vs. the Colonels 1967–1974:
a Controversial Relationship

57
Nikos Papanastasiou
Solidarity and Realpolitik?
Chancellor Willy Brandt, the Colonels in
Greece and the Dictatorships of the South

69
Hans Peter Schunk
On Hair Police, Political Pornographers and
Devourers of Communists: German
Press about the Greek Military Dictatorship
(1967–1974)

93
Frank Bösch
Greek-German Protest:
Public Commitment against Greece's
Dictatorship in the Federal Republic

117
Antonis Sarantidis
The Greek Students' Resistance
against the Junta in Western Europe:
The Case of European Student Conferences (1967–1971)

137
Dimitrios Garris
Alekos Panagoulis: The Genesis
of an Anti-Dictatorship Hero (1968–1976)

151
Loukas Bartatilas
Solidarity Networks in Architecture:
Akademie der Künste
and Ioannis Despotopoulos

161
About the authors

Preface

The Archive of Social Democracy (*Archiv der sozialen Demokratie – AdsD*) of the Friedrich-Ebert-Stiftung in Bonn and the Contemporary Social History Archives (ASKI) in Athens are connected by a fruitful and long-standing cooperation. Both institutions conduct historical research and debates on left-wing social history and labour movements.

In recent years, AdsD and ASKI have successfully worked on a number of joint projects. In August 2017, AdsD and ASKI celebrated the opening of the touring exhibition titled "Solidarity and Resistance: German-Greek Relations during Greek Military Dictatorship 1967–1974" (*Solidarität und Widerstand. Deutsch-Griechische Beziehungen während der griechischen Militärdiktatur 1967–1974*) in Berlin. Then, in April 2018, the exhibition made its way to Greece and was opened in Athens. More than a dozen cities in both countries hosted the exhibition in the subsequent months. The project was funded by the German Federal Foreign Office within the context of the German-Greek future fund.

The exhibition project was initiated by Sigrid Skarpelis-Sperk, now honorary president of the Union of German-Greek Societies (*Vereinigung der Deutsch-Griechischen Gesellschaften e. V.* – VDGG). Her effort and dedication were crucial for the exhibition project. We would also like to thank Edelgard Buhlmann and Klaus Wettig whose support was vital, too.

Our partner ASKI deserves credit for a long-lasting and collegial cooperation. We would particularly like to thank Vangelis Karamanolakis who enriched our joint work with his foresight and background knowledge. The same holds true for his colleagues Kostis Karpozilos, Ioanna Vogli, Anda Kapola and Stathis Pavlopoulos. We would like to express our gratitude for their efforts.

Over time, a lot of people were involved in the German-Greek cooperation at the Archive of Social Democracy. Mike Woyke, Ursula Bitzegeio and Stefan Müller as heads of the Public History division of AdsD and Anja Kruke as head of AdsD carried responsibility in terms of project supervision. Stefan Müller was in charge of the realisation of the touring exhibition, supported by Mike Woyke. Jens Hettmann was entrusted with the tour planning, supported by Eva Váry. Ursula Bitzegeio and Joachim Schlütter organised the closing event of the touring exhibition in the form of an international academic workshop.

The present anthology is based on that workshop, entitled "Greek-German Relations During the Military Dictatorship in Greece (1967–1974)", which took place digitally on 6–7 October, 2020. In a two-day program, scholars from both Germany and Greece discussed new approaches to an interwoven Greek-German contemporary history. AdsD and ASKI would like to thank all panellists for their valuable contributions to our ongoing academic discussions, especially those who turned their oral contributions into papers for this book project. Due to a variety of circumstances, most of the articles in this anthology happen to have been written by men. The editors are aware of and regret this imbalance in terms of gender. We would like to express our general encouragement for women pursuing academic careers. Having noticed, with great interest, that young female scholars have embarked on historical research in the field of German-Greek contemporary history, we look forward to giving their contributions an equal platform again in future projects.

Chrysa Vachtsevanou accepted the task of editorial work for this anthology and has to be given credit for the content-related supervision of the contributions. Her work and effort have been vital for their publication. Stefan Zeppenfeld of AdsD managed the book project and communications with the parties involved in the publication process. Julia Dalhoff and Christine Brocks put finishing touches on the articles.

The foreign office of the Friedrich-Ebert-Stiftung in Athens covered all expenses of the anthology. We cordially thank our colleagues in Greece, Christos Katsioulis, Ulrich Stock, Arne Schildberg, Monika Berg, Angeliki Emmanouilidou and Stefanos Spiliotopoulos for their support, generosity and patience.

The articles by Chrysa Vachtsevanou, Hans Peter Schunk and Frank Bösch were published in the German journal *Zeitschrift für Politik*, issue 3/2022.[1]

Stefan Zeppenfeld
Archiv der sozialen Demokratie
Bonn, July 2022

---

[1] Zeitschrift für Politik (ZfP), Heft 3/2022, Baden-Baden: Nomos.

Chrysa Vachtsevanou,
Vangelis Karamanolakis

Introduction

The period of the military dictatorship in Greece (1967–1974) is retrospectively considered to be one of the most important chapters for the relationship between Germany and Greece because of the movement that developed on West-German soil against the colonels – a movement based on the strong presence of Greek immigrants in the Federal Republic of Germany, the support of a large part of West-German public opinion and the active support of the first post-war SPD government, under Willy Brandt.

West Germany was the engine of Greek resistance in Europe: the country hosted the most numerous and largest Greek anti-dictatorship organisations across the political spectrum, with highly visible activities and a considerable impact on German and international public opinion. Dozens of magazines and newspapers published in Greek and German criticized the dictatorial Greek regime. German trade unions, clubs and Greek-German civic associations, student organisations protested against the Greek junta. The Federal Government supported the Greek struggle, worked for the release of resistance activists imprisoned in Greece and issued 'alien's passports' to individuals whose Greek citizenship had been revoked by the regime in Athens.

During this period, personal networks and political connections between Germans and Greeks were established, many of which exist until today. Many of the Greeks who supported and were organised in the resistance against military rule in the Federal Republic returned to Greece after the end of the dictatorship and later assumed important functions in politics and society – such as former President of Greece Karolos Papoulias, and former Prime Minister Konstantinos Simitis.

On the one hand, we cannot understand Greek-German relations without considering the internal developments in the two countries – the establishment of a dictatorial regime in Greece and the election of an SPD government in power in West Germany. On the other hand, this relationship forms part of a wider field of international relations in the framework of the Cold War. The two countries were part of the same Cold War camp: they were both members of NATO; West Germany was one of the founders of the European Economic Community (EEC) while Greece was trying to become a member. Moreover, international developments such as the oil crisis of 1973, influenced the political choices of the two countries. On a non-governmental level, there were networks of citizens between the two countries, connected with international social movements of the time. Events such as those of May '68 and the activities of the West German youth movement became catalysts for many European countries, while phenomena such as post-war economic and labour migration created strong networks of communication among the citizens of different states.

Indeed, we cannot understand the anti-dictatorial movement in West Germany unless we link it to Greek economic migration into the country. The economic growth of West Germany was a powerful incentive for attracting foreign workers to the country. Meanwhile, for economically devastated post-war Greece, emigration abroad was a crucial outlet, as it relieved the volatile situation of a large labour force, while at the same time providing valuable foreign exchange from abroad through remittances.

The 1960 bilateral recruitment agreement triggered a huge wave of migration from Greece to Germany: by 1967, approximately 350,000 Greek workers, men and women, were living in West Germany. They were young, poorly educated, and coming mostly from rural areas.

Soon, their communities set up important networks between themselves and German society: political, religious and trade-union associations.

Seven Years with the "Phoenix": A short Chronicle of the Greek Junta

21st April 1967: at six o'clock in the morning, the Greek people were informed through a radio statement by an army spokesman that the military had taken power in the country and that certain articles of the constitution had been suspended. A few days after the coup, the new cabinet was formed by the three leading personalities of the Greek dictatorship: Colonel Georgios Papadopoulos took over the Ministry of State and the general coordination of government policy, Brigadier Stylianos Pattakos the Ministry of the Interior, and Colonel Nikolaos Makarezos the Ministry of Economy. The new government was thus largely comprised of generals who had been politically socialised within an anti-communist military system. Their goal was to 'return Greece to its former glory', to rise like a phoenix from the ashes', and therefore they had prepared for long-term rule of their regime from the onset. Nevertheless, through various measures, such as the 1968 constitutional referendum, they tried to convince the public that their presence in the Greek political landscape was short-term and that democracy would return as soon as possible.

Among the first measures taken by the military government was the imprisonment of former politicians, communists and democrats. Prime Minister Panagiotis Kanellopoulos, leader of the conservative party, was the first to be arrested and placed under house arrest. Georgios Papandreou, head of the Center Union (Enosis Kentrou), was detained in a military hospital and his son, Andreas Papandreou, head of the Panhellenic Socialist Movement (PASOK party) after 1974, was imprisoned. The leadership of the Left but also journalists, trade unionists, local government officials – a total of more than 6,000 mainly left-wing citizens were arrested. Most of them were soon moved to exile camps on the island of Gyaros. In general, the repressive measures taken by the colonels during the period of the junta corresponded to the usual ones of contemporary military dictatorships: arrests, deportations, censorship, interrogations, torture and bans on assembly were part of everyday political life for the opposition. Decisive for the perpetuation of military dictatorship was the restriction of the freedom of the press.

During the first years of the Greek dictatorship, the regime's surveillance was established in almost all areas of public and private life. Attempts at pushback were isolated as most of the few resistance organisations within the country were dismantled by the security service. The regime's political opponents were arrested, tortured and then sentenced to long prison terms. This first period would end with Greece's withdrawal from the Council of Europe in 1969 due to the complaints against the country for human rights violations. The false image of 'liberalisation' that the regime attempted to project abroad, claiming that the situation in Greece had been normalised, led to a new anti-dictatorship movement: the student movement. After 1971, students initiated high-visibility strikes and protests, initially focusing on student demands. Soon, however, their struggle turned into a movement against the dictatorship, demanding the return of democracy. This movement peaked in the occupation of the Law school in February 1973, and the Athens Polytechnic uprising (14–17 November 1973), which cost the lives of dozens of citizens due to the violent intervention of the junta. The uprising of the Polytechnic University contributed to the replacement of Papadopoulos in an internal coup by Dimitrios Ioannidis, previously commander of the military police. Unlike Papadopoulos, Ioannidis wanted to remain largely invisible in public during his entire time in power, which is why he did not assume any official office in the military government.

Ioannnidis' coup was intended to mark the beginning of the end of the dictatorship. After all, he broke with the legend that the junta was a united idealistic bloc with the goal of 'curing' Greece of corruption and mismanagement. This weakened the junta, especially internally, as popular support dwindled and fewer and fewer parts of the military stood behind the government. From then on, the army was seen as fragmented and in disarray, even as it continued to present itself to the outside world as confident and expansionist. The real reason for the end of the military dictatorship was the role of the military leadership in organising the coup against the government of Cyprus and the subsequent occupation of the island's north by Turkish troops. Due to the junta government's obvious complicity in the destabilisation of Cyprus, and its inability to prevent the Turkish invasion of the island, the dictatorship lost its power. After the military leadership decided to dismiss the Ioannidis administration, they handed over the reins to an interim civilian government headed by the former Prime Minister, Konstantinos Karamanlis.

Students and workers in West Germany: Greek expats against colonels

In West Germany, as in the rest of Europe, a series of associations and movements were formed out of solidarity with the Greek people. These associations successfully contributed to informing and influencing public opinion, organising events and concerts, publishing anti-dictatorship material and financing resistance groups. Operating on different levels, these groups tried to establish a discourse to counter the colonels' propaganda by denouncing cases of torture in Greece, publishing lists with thousands of political prisoners, and providing information about resistance activity within Greece. All of this information was silenced by the junta within the country but publicised internationally thanks to the networks of Greeks around the world, with great impact on public opinion.

From the first moment after the coup d'état of 21 April 1967, networks of Greek workers in Germany organised themselves, playing a significant role in informing German public opinion about the situation in their country – as reflected in the massive protests immediately following the takeover. Among other reasons, this was due to the pre-existing local organisations of Greek political parties and networks abroad, which had been keenly interested in potential voters in the years before the coup. The most highly organised political network amongst the immigrants was on the political Left. Since after the Greek civil war (1946–49) the communist party was banned, the legal expression of the Left in Greece was the Unified Democratic Left party (EDA). Together with its youth organisation, Lambrakis Democratic Youth, the EDA built a political network in West Germany. Another organisation with an important number of Greek expatriates in Germany among its ranks was the Centre Union, the party that aimed to occupy the political space between right and left under the leadership of Georgios Papandreou. Many of these organisations were transformed during the junta period due to a number of factors, including the split of the Greek communist party in February 1968, the creation in the same month of the Patriotic Anti-Dictatorial Front by Andreas Papandreou, and the formation of many Greek New Left organisations in West Germany. The result was the establishment of a large number of Greek anti-dictatorship organisations, mainly from the Left and Centre, which were primarily directed at Greek expatriates, linking their action against the junta with their political.

A separate facet consists of the anti-dictatorship activities of Greek students who moved to Germany for graduate or post-graduate studies. West Germany had been a destination for Greek academics and students before, in the 19th century – then supported by the Bavarian Wittelsbach dynasty. A remarkable number of Greeks attended German universities during the 1950s and '60s in fields such as law and literature, and some remained in the country to pursue professional careers. Following the example of their German peers, some of them were organised in primary-level associations and set up their own higher-level organisation, the Federation of Greek Student Unions of West Germany and West-Berlin. When the junta seized power, Greek anti-regime students set up groups to bring pressure to bear on German politicians for an international denunciation and isolation of the Greek junta. Often, their experience and knowledge of the way the public sphere worked in West Germany contributed to their success.

Developments such as the de facto suspension of the Accession Agreement to the European Economic Community, the eviction of the junta from the Council of Europe in 1969, and the arms embargo against the Greek state were also due to uncountable denunciations in international fora and pressure exerted by Greeks abroad. The Federal Republic offered a hospitable refuge to many anti-regime Greeks who found shelter and employment there. The case of Georgios A. Mangakis is exemplary: having studied law in Germany, Mangakis was teaching as an associate professor at the Law School of Athens from which he was fired by the dictatorial regime. He was also arrested for his anti-dictatorship activity. In 1972, while he was imprisoned, the University of Heidelberg appointed him as a professor. After strong pressure from international public opinion, Mangakis was released from prison for health reasons and was able to resettle in Heidelberg.

Greek anti-dictatorship organisations abroad supported the Greek resistance on the ground, offering economic assistance and lending an international dimension to the national struggle. Still, the anti-dictatorship movement in Germany could not have succeeded without the support of German public opinion which proved very sensitive to the Greek cause. In a decade of flourishing social movements, the military rule in Greece was seen by many as yet another bastion of tyranny and authoritarianism in a global struggle spanning Chile, the Iberian Peninsula, and Vietnam. For some, Greece symbolised the birthplace of democracy due to its history. The demand that Germany denounce the Greek regime was linked with Germany's own broader foreign policy and the obligation, 22 years after the end of World War II, to act as a defender of democracy and freedom.

Thanks to the mobilisation of Greeks in Germany, the Greek cause found sympathy in many institutions, first and foremost in the German political parties. Of critical importance in this respect was the stance of the SPD and of Willy Brandt as chancellor. Although the Federal Republic, like the other European countries, never broke off its relations with the military junta, the SPD's positive stance vis-à-vis Greek anti-regime forces played a determining role in terms of economic support to the struggle against the dictatorship. SPD's stance was not always unanimous or monolithic, especially regarding issues of governmental policy and diverging interests and strategies. Nevertheless, within the climate of resistance in the wake of May '68 in West Germany, there was active support of the Greek question by German New Left organisations. At the same time, German trade unions played a decisive role in supporting the Greek anti-dictatorship struggle, as did dozens of joint initiatives of Greek and German citizens throughout the country. This support was decisive in opening a new chapter in Greek-German relations after the traumatic experience of World War II and the occupation of Greece by Nazi troops.

All in all, the discussion about the anti-dictatorship struggle in Germany cannot be separated from the experience of immigration and the way the latter was embedded in the wider changes of the 1960s. For instance, albeit fearing and mistrusting trade-union representation, workers were almost obliged to join labour unions, which cared about protecting their rights. 150,000 Greeks joined German trade unions. Due to their migration, Greeks abroad, living in an environment of tremendous change and a burning demand for democracy, developed stronger feelings in regard to the military junta. In fact, the central question which dominated their discussions – as evidenced by articles in the anti-regime press, workers' personal correspondence and protocols of their meetings – was what would happen the day after the fall of the junta regime. An analysis of these discussions by Greek migrants could also give some perspectives on studying the anti-dictatorship struggle in Germany: As a big laboratory for all Greek political forces, of fermenting ideas, a meeting point for people having arrived from different, opposing political paths, forged out of the traumas of the 1940s, to join forces against the junta.

Conclusions: Quo vadis ... public history?

Migration and totalitarian regimes have been some of the major features of the 20th century. The Greek dictatorship coincided with a turning point in the country's history when migration and urbanisation signalled, to a great extent, the end of a traditional way of life, the dismantling of old hierarchies and power structures. Young emigrants, men and women, became recipients of multi-faceted information and stimuli, inevitably leading them to make comparisons between the old and new which often made them long for change. In this context and in the light of their new experiences, Greek immigrants in Germany and Europe in general took a negative stance on military rule. Their dream of returning to the homeland was accompanied by a wish for normalcy in political life, by the demand to live in a country not constantly in a state of emergency.

In this context, it is appropriate to pay homage to the thousands of Greek immigrants and German citizens who fought against the Greek Junta and supported the anti-dictatorship movement – but also to the German institutions (political parties, trade unions, churches, solidarity groups and committees) that supported the Greeks, recalling an almost forgotten page of their common history, based on solidarity and democratic support. It is a shared duty for both Germans and Greeks to deal with their common past: to historicise and grapple with the darkest and most difficult sides of it, but also to praise the bright moments and preserve them in collective memory for the next generations.

This anthology is part of a broader cooperation between two archives in Germany and Greece. The Archive of Social Democracy (AdsD) and the Library of the Friedrich-Ebert-Stiftung in Bonn are central repositories for sources of all kinds on the history of German Social Democracy, as well as international and German labour and social movements. The Greek Archive of Contemporary Social History (ASKI), located in Athens, is the leading Greek archival institution for the history of the Greek Left, for political and social movements and Greek social history. Both ASKI and FES carry out a number of public history projects and activities that enrich historical awareness and the collective memory of different identity groups.

Obviously, it is not possible to cover all aspects of the bilateral relations and the junta opposition within a single anthology. The aim of this volume is to open the dialogue on Greek-German relations during the period 1967–74. This dialogue takes place in a multi-levelled field of study transcending the national history of each country in what we would call transnational history.

How controversial was the relationship between the Federal Republic of Germany and the Greek Colonels in the context of the Cold War? How did the Greek issue become a German issue, concerning the political conflicts within the SPD and even its full adoption by the German student movement? How did the German media perceive the Greek Junta? How did the anti-dictatorship protests of the Greek immigrants, students and press in the Federal Republic of Germany and in Europe emerge as a motor of protest, challenging and sometimes shaping German realpolitik and foreign policy? These are some of the main questions addressed in this volume. The genesis of individual symbolic figures like Alekos Panagoulis, who fought against the dictatorship, as well as the (largely unknown) struggle of the architect Ioannis Despotopoulos, are distinctive, noteworthy stories of this period – aspects of which are also presented within this anthology.

It is high time that scholars and institutions in both countries take steps and develop oral and public history projects, aiming to systematically collect testimonies from Greek and German individuals and witnesses of this period. At the same time, it is vital to bring together archival material from public records, political parties and agencies, as well as from physical persons – before precious sources are forever lost.

Chrysa Vachtsevanou

The Cradle of Democracy "in a Plaster Cast"[1]: West German Foreign Policy towards the Greek Military Dictatorship (1967–1974)

Apart from the First World War, during which both countries fought on opposite sides, and the occupation of Greece by the Wehrmacht in the Second World War, Germany and Greece have had long-standing ties of friendship during the most part of the last 200 years. One example for the close economic and social ties is the migration movement during the 1960s and 1970s, when hundreds of thousands of Greeks emigrated to the Federal Republic of Germany. This period, which was significantly shaped by the bipolar world order and the Cold War, coincided with the military rule in Greece (1967–1974). In retrospect, these years are considered the central phase of good relations between Germans and Greeks. They were, as one hypothesis suggests, the cornerstone of today's bilateral relations.[2]

When exploring the facets of the bilateral relations over the course of the military dictatorship in greater detail, it becomes clear that West German foreign policy was much more ambivalent than support for the Greek opposition suggests. There was, without a doubt, broad support for the fight against the dictatorship, particularly by trade unions and ordinary people. The Federal government also used official channels to restore the rule of law and democracy in Greece. However, unlike other states, such as the Scandinavian countries, West Germany did not impose sanctions including a reduction or breaking off of trade relations.[3] It is striking that in some cases economic and political relations with the Greek military regime became even closer. In this context, *Realpolitik* interests and strategic goals of federal foreign policy towards Athens were of decisive importance.

What was the social political basis of Greek-West German relations during the military dictatorship? Which obstacles and alliances shaped the bilateral relations between the two countries? Or, which ambivalences become visible in the West German policy towards the autocratic regime during the seven-year military dictatorship by looking at Greek-West German relations? How did the change of government in 1969 and the chancellorship of Willy Brandt affect the foreign political position of the Federal Republic? This paper seeks to address these questions with the aim of contributing to the topical discourse on Greek-German memory culture.

Riots, uprisings and putsches in Greece: a country at political unrest

Pavlos Bakojannis, political scientist and, during the Greek military dictatorship, editor-in-chief of the Greek department at the *Bayerische Rundfunk*, a Bavarian public broadcaster, counted as many as 42 riots, uprisings and putsches between 1830, the formation of the Greek state, and the military putsch on 21 April 1967. According to Bakojannis, the reasons for these rebellions against the Greek state were manifold, with some of them grown out of "genuine concern about Greece's wellbeing and many out of professional dissatisfaction and personal jealousies".[4]

Over the entire post-war period, Greece was a deeply divided country. While Germany turned into the centre of the Cold War,[5] Greece became the "Eastern flank"[6] of Europe and the Western defence alliance. Greece's geographical location played a major role in NATO's fight against the so-called communist threat – with the Americans' anti-communist stance rubbing off on the Greek military. Alongside the Church, the Military was the most influential organisation in Greek society during the period after the Second World War and became the main representative of the anti-communist doctrine in Greece: in collaboration with NATO, the Greek government drew up an emergency defence plan against a potential communist attack, the so called "Prometheus Plan"[7], which had been in the drawers of the military from the 1950s.[8]

The developments in state and society reflected the intentions and positions of the victors of the civil war: the conservative-royalist government. The country turned into a strongly conservative and anti-communist state. In the process, a system emerged with the aim of repressing not only left-wing revolutionary but also liberal and social democratic currents in the population under the pretext of the fight against Communism. During the initial post-civil war years, the king, the army, the police, and the Greek secret service had a greater impact on politics than parliament and government.[9] The political situation was dominated by the perennial conflict between right-wing conservative and left-wing liberal politicians, the king's constant interferences with the affairs of elected governments, a weak economy and conflicts with Turkey about the future of Cyprus. All these factors ultimately resulted in growing political instability and unstable governments.[10]

Elections were planned for 28 May 1967, with the left-liberal Andreas Papandreou,[11] whose popularity had been constantly growing from 1965, being expected to win again.[12] In order to prevent a left-liberal government under his leadership, which at the time was not an "acceptable alternative"[13] for both the economic and political elite in Greece and the influential partner USA, a small group of generals and officers staged a coup d'état against government and king during the night of 20 April 1967.

For Colonel Georgios Papadopoulos, leader of the putsch and minister president of the junta cabinet from December 1967, an anti-communist stance and loyalty towards NATO were paramount.[14] He was, however, well aware that Greece's potential and broadly desired accession to the European Community presupposed the demilitarisation and democratisation of the government in Athens. For this reason, he ruled out this development at the latest after 1969.[15] In April 1969, he already replied to his adversaries abroad, who demanded the return to democracy, that "the revolution in Greece has turned the country from being dominated by the mob into a haven of calm within an unsettled Europe".[16]

The coup of the Greek Colonels and the Federal government's reaction

The international public was very much concerned about the political situation in Greece, which greatly influenced Greece's international relations, at least at the beginning of the dictatorship. Foreign embassies in Athens, including the West German one under the leadership of the conservative Oskar Schlitter, had been taken by surprise by the putsch, even though the Federal Republic's intelligence services were well connected with Greece.[17]

On the day of the coup, Schlitter and other diplomatic representatives had been provided with "only very little and random information about the tumultuous events",[18] as telephone and teletext connections were disrupted and embassies were unable to get in contact with the governments of their respective countries. While initially economic and security political interests did not appear to be under threat in Greece, the Western world – and Bonn in particular – was deeply worried about the events and the blatant violation of democratic principles and the rule of law. However, in view of Greece's geopolitical position and the communist threat, the West German diplomats in Athens responded with caution.[19]

In any case, the question of diplomatically recognising the military regime did not arise during the initial months because Greek King Konstantin was still the legitimate head of state.[20] During the first weeks after the putsch, Oskar Schlitter assumed the military regime would soon transition into a democratic government and snap elections would be held, while he was rather sympathetic towards the regime's announced reform plans against communism and corruption.[21] One month after the coup he reported that "technical preparations and the implementation of the announced reforms [...]" would take "a certain and unpredictable length of time".[22] Especially with an eye to NATO obligations, Schlitter always expressed an optimistic view of the military government in his reports to the Federal government during that time.[23]

Equally optimistic about the Colonels' plans to restore democracy was the Hamburg businessman Erik Blumenfeld (CDU), the first well-known federal politician who visited Greece after the coup. After his return he explained in an interview with the weekly *Die Zeit* that, although not sympathising with the putschists, he nevertheless "understood" the situation of the military government and had no doubt that it would do everything in its power to adopt a new constitution and hold free elections in due course.[24] Blumenfeld took the view that "the regime deserved a chance" and pointed out that "NATO is a defence organisation, not a political alliance".[25]

In contrast to some CDU/CSU members, Social Democrats and Liberals had a much more critical view of the putschists. In a Bundestag debate on the situation in Greece, Foreign Minister Willy Brandt (SPD) voiced great concerns about the abolition of basic rights and the departure from democracy:

> "Our only interest is humanity, the rule of law and democracy, but also, related to this, the credibility of organisations that we are a part of. The Federal government is aware of the statement issued by the king of Greece about the return to the rule of law. Especially our friendship with the Greek people makes us wish that this will happen very soon and go well."[26]

The FDP shared the Social Democrats' worries and criticised the government under Federal Chancellor Kurt Georg Kiesinger (CDU).

Thus, the Liberal parliamentary party of the Bundestag urged the government:

> "make use of all reasonable political, diplomatic and economic means available, both in the context of the Council of Europe and the Atlantic Pact, to ensure that Greece at least guarantees personal freedom, legal protection and the UN declaration of human rights, as the threat of a communist revolution no longer appears imminent."[27]

In retrospect it can be ascertained that the Federal Republic de facto continued diplomatic relations with the Greek military regime after 12 June 1967, that is after the Greek journalist Basil Mathiopoulos, who sought asylum in the West German embassy, had left Greece for the Federal Republic.[28] When in December 1967 the counter-coup of the king, who was still head of state, failed, most Western countries initially severed official diplomatic contacts with the Colonels. Eventually, the new military government of Greece officially gained international recognition in early 1968.[29]

Greek opposition via West-German microphones

In Greece an effective opposition was unable to establish itself due to repressions, arrests and torture through the regime. However, many Greeks who lived abroad set up resistance groups against the junta. In particular, organised resistance in the Federal Republic played a major role in this context, experiencing a significant boost in the wake of social change and developments at universities and in trade unions in the context of the 1968 movement.[30] The tools of the opposition were radio broadcasts critical of the regime and publications that also, at least in some cases, circulated in Greece as well as speeches of politicians and intellectuals in exile and protest demonstrations.[31]

As early as 1964, two radio programmes in the Greek language were broadcasted daily from the Federal Republic: a 40-minute programme of the *Deutsche Welle* (DW) and a 45-minute programme of the *Bayerische Rundfunk* (BR).[32] These two broadcasters, and primarily the DW "propagating German politics and culture abroad",[33] played a significant role for the development of Greek resistance against the military government. As public broadcasters, they often trod a thin line between critical and diplomatic coverage. While BR programmes mainly addressed Greek migrant workers in the Federal Republic, DW reportages were also broadcasted in Greece and thus addressed the broader Greek population in their home country.

In August 1967, with an eye to the DW coverage of Greece, Ministerialdirigent Alexander Böker, a high-ranking official in the Foreign Office, explained it should not be withheld from the Greek public that the German population very much wished for a return to Democracy in Greece.[34] Yet the superiors of the Greek journalists at the DW urged them to remain impartial after the coup. Indeed, the oppositional coverage of the DW only started two years later, in May 1969, after the election of Walter Steigner (SPD) as new general director of the DW. The Greek programme was extended to one hour and moved to a better timeslot. The Greek editorial office often aired critical reports by Pavlos Bakojannis, head of the Greek department of the BR, who worked together closely with *Der Spiegel* correspondent in Athens, Kostas Tsatsaronis.[35] In addition to the contributions of Tsatsaronis and the BR, the DW also broadcasted various anonymous analyses of the domestic situation in Greece.[36] These informative reports and anti-regime commentaries by the Greek editorial team played a similar role to the BBC coverage in Germany during the Second World War.[37]

The increasing mobilisation of Greeks in the Federal Republic was a source of growing concern for the Colonels. More and more organisations, associations and institutions in West Germany participated in a critical discussion of the military dictatorship. As a result, the Greek government in Athens even put pressure on Greek communities and exiles in the Federal Republic, either by intimidation attempts of government officials, espionage or the threat of issuing entry bans to Greece.³⁸

At the same time, the Greek broadcasts were targeted by the Colonels' censorship. As early as two weeks after the coup, the military leadership criticised that background reports on the putsch and the military government by foreign media were false and that oppositional Greeks had too much influence on the public perception abroad.³⁹ Simultaneously, the Greek ambassador to Bonn, Alexis Kyrou,⁴⁰ informed the head of foreign programmes at the BR, Gerhard Bogner, that he would cease the collaboration with the Greek programme entirely – he hoped "that someday the programmes for Greek workers might regain their old objectivity".⁴¹

The increasingly critical coverage of the DW resulted in several open conflicts between Greece and the Federal Republic. After negotiations between the West German and the Greek editorial offices and following the suggestion of the Greek government spokesman Stamatopoulos, it was decided in February 1972 that, unlike before, all Greek contributions of the DW were to be translated into German and approved by West German superiors before airing them.⁴² The Greek DW journalists considered these measures preventive censorship.⁴³ However, Danae Coulmas, who worked at the Greek department of the DW at the time, pointed out that the Greek journalists and their superiors had to make such compromises to continue airing their programmes in Greece. "We had to be loyal to our German superiors, who in turn did everything so that we would keep our freedoms"⁴⁴

Despite several attempts of the military government to influence the DW coverage via the West German embassy and the Federal government, it largely remained critical of the dictatorship during its entire existence. In the first months of 1974, the programmes of the DW and the *Bayerische Rundfunk* were the only reliable sources about the political situation in Greece due to the comprehensive press censorship in Greece.⁴⁵

Federal governments between economic interests, Realpolitik and value-based politics

Economic collaboration in the form of trade, West German capital assistance, the recruitment of Greek workers from 1960 onwards as well as granting technical assistance to Greece played a profound role in establishing bilateral relations between both countries in the post-war period. Economic collaboration and the recruitment agreement in 1960 professionalised the cooperation between the Federal Labour Ministry and the West German embassy to Athens with Greek authorities.[46]

In the eyes of the Federal government, Greece, provided substantial chances to expand the West German industry in the 1950s, despite only being a small market. The amount of West German goods exported to Greece remained relatively stable throughout the entire post-war period – compared with exports from the USA and the UK, which declined during the same period of time.[47] The Federal Republic became Greece's most important economic and trading partner.[48] Alongside military strategic considerations and Willy Brandt's foreign political principles, these economic relations played a crucial role for the relationship between the various Federal governments and the Greek military regime. The Federal Republic was connected with Greece through three important agreements[49] and for this reason, Bonn was keen not to let the political unease about the situation in Greece affect economic relations.[50] This position hardly changed during the entire duration of the Greek military dictatorship, neither under Kiesinger as chancellor nor under Brandt.[51]

Overall, Bonn's foreign policy towards Athens was torn: a balancing act between geostrategic, economic and idealistic considerations – and there was probably no other politician who internalised this conflict more clearly than Willy Brandt. Furthermore, no other cabinet minister played a more important role in the bilateral relations than Brandt, who was Foreign Minister of the Grand Coalition during the military coup and elected chancellor in 1969. The principles of "change through rapprochement" and "dédtente in Europe"[52] famously marked his foreign policy and were crucial for his position towards the Greek military government.[53]

Other Western European countries, however, were less hesitant in their approach towards the Greek military regime. Due to the detention and torture of potential dissidents that had become publicly known, Denmark, Sweden and Norway filed an official complaint against Greece at the Council of Europe in Summer 1967. In September 1967, another complaint was lodged with the European Commission on Human Rights for violations of the European Convention on Human Rights. A special commission was established to inquire into the human rights situation in Greece. The Federal government, fully in line with its general position, remained cautious regarding the question of how the Council of Europe should deal with Greece, avoiding potential economic repercussions and consequences for NATO.[54]

Even before the meeting of the Minister Committee of the Council of Europe in Paris on 12 December 1969, there was an agreement that Greece could not retain full membership of the Council. While many SPD members took the view that Greece's exclusion from the Council of Europe could only be the beginning of further sanctions, several CDU parliamentarians felt vindicated in their objections to the Council's policy towards Greece. They were worried Greece might break away from NATO.[55]

First debates on the impact of the coup on Greece's membership of NATO emerged as early as 1967 in the context of discussions on Greece's potential exclusion from the Council of Europe.[56] Looking at the Federal government's view concerning Greece's position in NATO and military assistance for Greece, it is striking how West German foreign policy was torn between *Realpolitik* and value-based policies. On the one hand, the Federal government by no means wanted to isolate Greed internationally[57] or, even worse, push it out of NATO and towards a closer partnership with the Soviet Union.[58] In addition, there were West German economic interests to consider. Above all, the French armament industry was to be prevented from taking away commissions from West German arms manufacturers in the long term.[59] On the other hand, Social Democrats were adamant to show the junta and the world that the Federal government's foreign policy was not only strategic but also value-based.[60]

In his memoirs *Erinnerungen*, Willy Brandt wrote considering human rights and democracy, that he "applied strict criteria in the West and where governments wished to be considered part of the West"[61] – "Europe cannot be seen in isolation from human rights; and anyone who wants to belong to Europe must maintain them."[62]

Willy Brandt's position towards the Greek military regime was, on the one hand, shaped by the geopolitical situation of the time and, on the other, by his moral worldview and personal experiences during the Third Reich.[63] This is another reason why relations between Greek resistance organisations and the Federal government, particularly under Brandt's chancellorship (1969–1974), were considered good. Willy Brandt and other cabinet ministers were on friendly terms with several Greek dissidents, which was reflected in the commitment for individual resistance fighters. The most prominent example is probably the support for the journalist Basil Mathiopoulos, who worked in the Federal Republic. At the time of the coup, Mathiopoulos, together with the journalist Thilo Koch and a TV team, were in Athens for a shooting for *Norddeutsche Rundfunk*, a public broadcaster based in Hamburg. The Greek journalist – like 6,000 other dissidents – was persecuted by the regime, but with Koch's help he was able to seek asylum in the West German embassy. After Brandt's personal intervention, Mathiopoulos returned to the Federal Republic on 11 June 1967.[64]

As chancellor, Brandt continued his efforts to help people persecuted by the Greek regime, although he thought that he 'was given more credit than was due' for his assistance.[65] And yet, in general the situation in Greece hardly changed: while some dissidents were released, repressions against others were tightened.[66] However, this ended abruptly with the so called "Mangakis affair", which made relations between Greece and West Germany reach a temporary low. The Athens-based lawyer and university professor Georgios Mangakis was given a prison sentence for his stance against the dictatorship. With the support of the Federal government and Ambassador Peter Limbourg, who became Oskar Schlitter's successor in 1969, he could be flown from the NATO military airport in Athens to the Federal Republic in April 1972, when he was temporarily out of prison due to health reasons. As a result, the Greek military government demanded Limbourg's dismissal.[67] The Mangakis affair substantially affected Greek-West German relations until the end of the dictatorship, touching the core of the Federal government's ambivalent position towards both the regime in Athens and the democratic opposition: "In the beginning, two different impulses crossed on the German side: the humanitarian and the strategic."[68]

Brandt was much more critical towards the regime than he could publicly express in his capacity as foreign minister and chancellor.[69] Thus, he often hid his criticism of Greece between the lines. In the already mentioned 1967 Bundestag debate, critics in his own party attacked him for not sufficiently condemning the regime. He responded that his official remarks did not reflect his personal thoughts but the position of the German Federal government and had to be understood accordingly.[70] Although Brandt did not demand Greece's exclusion from the Council of Europe, he was convinced it was paramount for the Greek government to show respect for international norms and values.

As chancellor, Brandt expressed his criticism of the Greek regime not least through his media-effective appearances and his imagery, conveying that he only communicated with Athens concerning economic affairs and according to diplomatic protocol while avoiding any other contact. When, for example, his plane landed in Athens for a stopover after a visit in Turkey in 1969, Brandt did not leave the plane to avoid a meeting with representatives of the military government.[71] Political opponents, particularly from the CSU, criticised this incident as being adverse to West German economic interests.[72] Yet Brandt's behaviour hardly threatened political and economic relations: the Greek Colonels recognised Brandt's support for Greek dissidents and his distance from the military regime were necessary to pacify critical voices in the SPD and the German public in general.[73]

However, the CSU was worried that due to the Greek opposition in the Federal Republic and the "hostile attitude of the Federal government, above all of the Foreign Minister"[74] – Willy Brandt – trade with Greece would be suffering. Franz Sackmann, state secretary in the Bavarian Ministry for Economic Affairs and foundation member of the CSU, voiced his concerns in June 1969 "with regard to the increasing deterioration of the traditionally good Greek-German relations" and "the economic and political damage".[75] In early October 1969, shortly before the establishment of the social-liberal coalition and Greece's foreseeable exit from the Council of Europe, Sackmann went to Athens and informed the military regime that Bavaria would, in future, pursue a policy towards Greece independently from Bonn.[76] According to a report in *Der Spiegel*, Sackmann saw his visit to Athens as "a corrective to Willy Brandt's foreign policy, which has damaged West German economic interests", and promised the Colonels Bavarian state loans.[77] [78] In addition, the Bavarian Minister President Fran Josef Strauß praised the Greek currency, the drachma, as "the most stable currency of the world today"[79] and claimed that the Colonels had turned Greece into a politically stable country.[80]

Half a year before the collapse of the military regime, the West German Ambassador to Athens, Dirk Onken, still stressed the necessity to be cautious. In a report on "Attentismus in Greece" from 25 January 1974, he portrayed the Greek regime as "a provisional government", which nonetheless "seems to have developed more resistance than previously expected". Along the lines of Papadopoulos' penchant for medical imagery, he described the situation in Greece as follows: "One attempts to correct the mistakes of the Papadopoulos regime, gag the dissatisfied public and keep one's future options open – all this is rather homoeopathy than surgery; there is little sign of serious diagnostics."[81] The European countries, the diplomat wrote, had "under these circumstances no choice but to wait and see. However, it seems advisable to keep in close contact with the Americans who at least have leverage in military terms (military assistance etc.)."[82]

As early as one month after the coup, Oskar Schlitter outlined the political guidelines that his successors, Peter Limbourg and Dirk Onken, as well as the majority of the Foreign Office would follow: "appeasement with nuances" – as was aptly coined by German-Greek historian Hagen Fleischer.[83]

Conclusion

As this article's analysis of West German-Greek relations during the Greek military dictatorship has shown, the role of internal as well as external factors is particularly important for researches of the Federal Republic's foreign political relationship with authoritarian regimes. Over the course of time under study, Federal governments strived, on the one hand, for a balance between the normative commitment for democracy and human rights and, on the other, vested foreign political and economic interests.

These interests were, to a certain extent, geostrategic but also the result of economic considerations. As a consequence, relations between the Federal Republic and Greece remained almost unchanged in the early days after the coup, as Bonn wanted to wait and see how the situation in Greece would develop. While leading politicians, particularly Social Democrats, repeatedly voiced criticisms of the developments in Athens, the Federal government reacted more cautiously. They did not want to jeopardise Greece's NATO membership, its association with the EEC and, above all, West Germany's position as Greece's most important trade partner.

The overall conclusion is that, even under the new Chancellor Willy Brandt, the Federal Republic's policy towards Greece from 1969 was marked by continuity – albeit with a slightly different focus – rather than radical change. This new focus can be explained by both Brandt's personal views and the position of many Social Democrats as well as the deteriorating situation in Greece during the early 1970s.

Chancellor Brandt's crucial point of departure was the desired balance between a personal commitment for dissidents in Greece and the Federal Republic' strategic interests. Only by considering the intense national and international pressure on the Brandt government and the chancellor himself can we understand their sometimes-ambiguous policy towards Greece. Nationally, particularly the CDU/CSU and West German businesses pushed the government to maintain good relations which was also in the Federal Republic's international interest as a close partner of the USA and for NATO's sake. At the same time, individual actors in West German society and the media urged the government for a punitive stance towards Athens.

In summary, Bonn did not adopt a clear-cut foreign policy towards Athens during the military dictatorship. The Federal governments balanced realistic considerations and normative aims; this cautious wait-and-see strategy remained in place until the collapse of the regime on 24 July 1974. When trying to chart the reasons for this position, the complexity of foreign political problems and the plethora of different actors come to the fore: who determined the political course of action depended on the situation at hand.

Translated from German into English by Christine Brocks

---

1   When the Greek dictator, Georgios Papadopoulos, first appeared in public at an international press conference on 21 April 1967, one week after the military putsch, he compared Greece to a patient who "needed a plaster cast". Quoted in Meletis Meletopoulos, *I diktatoria ton syntagmatarchon* [The Dictatorship of the Colonels] (Athens: Papazisis, 2008), 168. In his political speeches, Papadopoulos often used imagery seemingly inspired by medicine.

2   See on this Dimitris K. Apostolopoulos, "Epanaproseggisi kai simfiliosi: Apo thn eksomalinsi tou katochikou parelthontos stin koini drasi gia tin edraiosi tis dimokratias stin Ellada" [Rapprochement and Reconciliation: From the Normalization of the Occupation Past to Concerted Action Aiming at Strengthening Democracy in Greece (1950–1979)], in: Stratos N. Dordanas/Nikos Papanastasiou (eds.), *O makris ellinogermanikos eikostos aionas* [The

Long German-Greek Twentieth Century] (Thessaloniki: Epikentro, 2018) and, in greater detail, Dimitris K. Apostolopoulos, *Die griechisch-deutschen Nachkriegsbeziehungen* (Frankfurt a. M.: Peter Lang, 2004).

3 Arms deals in the context of the NATO Defence Assistance Programme played an important role for the increasing economic relations between both countries from the early 1960s onwards. The Federal Republic's first arms deliveries abroad started in the 1960s and developed on three levels: first as military assistance programmes for selected countries, second as a sale of surplus arms of the Bundeswehr – either by government bodies or private institutions to foreign armies – and third through contacts between West German companies and foreign governments. Cf. William Glenn Gray, "Waffen aus Deutschland? Bundestag, Rüstungshilfe und Waffenexport 1961 bis 1975," in: *Vierteljahrshefte für Zeitgeschichte*, vol. 64 (2016), no. 2, 328.

4 Pavlos Bakojannis, *Militärherrschaft in Griechenland* (Stuttgart: Kohlhammer, 1972).

5 Cf. Eckhard Jesse, "Die Bundesrepublik Deutschland und die deutsche Frage 1945 bis 1961," in: Andreas H. Apelt, Martin Gutzeit and Gerd Poppe (eds.), *Die deutsche Frage in der SBZ und DDR. Deutschlandpolitische Vorstellungen von Bevölkerung und Opposition 1945–1990* (Berlin: Metropol, 2010), 37.

6 Dean Acheson, Secretary of State of the Truman administration from 1949 to 1953, referred to Greece as the "Eastern flank of European defence". Cf. Dean Acheson, *Present at the Creation: My Years in the State Department* (New York: W. W. Norton, 1987), 569–70.

7 For more details on the "Prometheus Plan" see Alexis Papachelas, *O viasmos tis ellinikis dimokratias: o amerikanikos paragon, 1947–1967* [The Adulteration of Greek Democracy: the American Factor, 1947–1967] (Athens: Estia, 2000), 258–260.

8 A version of this Prometheus Plan was eventually used by officers around Georgios Papadopoulos for the seizure of power through the army in April 1967. Cf. Sotiris Rizas, *I elliniki politiki meta ton Emfylio: Koinovouleftismos kai Diktatoria* [Greek Politics after the Civil War: Parliamentarianism and Dictatorship] (Athens: Kastaniotis, 2008), 360.

9 Although the civil war is not a topic of this contribution, it must be stressed that its influence on 1960s politics was decisive. After the end of the war, the population was still divided. Communists and liberals were declared enemies of the state, which the Greek shadow state intended to fight with all available means. Within this shadow state, some relatively low-ranking militaries formed a special group of officers, the IDEA, who were assigned to reach higher positions within the army and create more political stability. Georgios Papadopoulos, the later leader of the Greek military government, was also a member of the IDEA. Cf. Rizas, *I elliniki politiki meta ton Emfylio*, 27–29.

10 On this see Spyros Linardatos, *Apo ton Emphilio stin Chounta* [From Civil War to Junta], vol. B (Athens: Papazisis, 1978) and Antonis Liakos, *O ellinikos 20os aionas* [The Greek Twentieth Century] (Athens: Polis, 2019).

11 For more details on Papandreou see Stan Draenos, *Andreas Papandreou – The Making of a Greek Democrat and Political Maverick* (New York: I. B. Tauris, 2012). On his policy see also Andreas Papandreou, *I Dimokratia sto Apospasma* [Democracy Put up Against the Wall] (Athens: Livanis, 2006).

12 Stephen Russeas summarises the most important factors during the crisis years in Greece (1965–1967) as follows: "For one thing, there was the time factor. [...] Time was increasingly running out – corresponding to the deadline for holding elections that was getting closer and closer. The other changing factor was Andreas Papandreou's popularity." Stephen Russeas, *Militärputsch in Griechenland oder Im Hintergrund der CIA* (Reinbek: Rowohlt, 1968), 54.

13 "Warning by Johnson to Greece is Denied," *New York Times*, 20 April 1967, 22.

14 Cf. "Neue Verfassung für Griechenland?," *Die Zeit* 12 May 1967.

15 Cf. Meletopoulos, *I diktatoria ton syntagmatarchon*, 314.

16 "Griechenland/Jahrestag: Schöne Demokratie," *Der Spiegel* 18/1969, 125.

17 Cf. Solon N. Grigoriadis, vol 9: *Istoria tis sygchronis Elladas 1941-1974: Chounta kai antistasi* [History of Modern Greece 1941-1974: Junta and Resistance] (Athens: Polaris, 2011), 146-7.

18 Cf. Basil P. Mathiopoulos, *Athen Brennt* (Darmstadt: Schneekluth, 1967), 52.

19 Cf. Apostolopoulos, *Die griechisch-deutschen Nachkriegsbeziehungen*, 318 and AAPD 20 May 1967, doc. no. 177, 767 and AAPD 24 August 1967, doc. no. 308, 1220.

20 Cf. Rizas, *I elliniki politiki meta ton Emfylio*, 437-9.

21 AAPD 20 May 1967, doc. no. 177, 767.

22 AAPD 24 August 1967, doc. no. 308, 1220, FN 5.

23 "The new government is certainly a more reliable NATO partner than its predecessors. While the latter started to increasingly adopt French ideas, the government today is beyond doubt a supporter of integration." Quoted in ibid. The major goal of the Federal Republic – apart from its own integration with the West – was to prevent international recognition of a second state on German soil – in the sense of the Hallstein doctrine. Cf. Kilian Werner, *Die Hallstein-Doktrin: Der diplomatische Krieg zwischen der BRD und der DDR 1955-1973*, (Berlin: Duncker und Humblot, 2001), 22-5.

24 "Doch Hoffnung für Griechenland?," *Die Zeit* 20 October 1967.

25 "Blumenfeld warnt Athener Junta," *Frankfurter Rundschau* 10 June 1968.

26 Willy Brandt, quoted in *Deutscher Bundestag*, 5. Wahlperiode, 126. Sitzung, Bonn 13 October 1967, 6335.

27 *Deutscher Bundestag*, 5. Wahlperiode, 126. Sitzung, Bonn 13 October 1967, 6373.

28 For more information on this see Basil P. Mathiopoulos, "Willy Brandt – Anmerkungen zu einem Freund," in: Bundeskanzler-Willy-Brandt-Stiftung [BWBS] (ed.), Schriftenreihe, issue 12 (Berlin: BWBS, 2005), 25.

29 Cf. Rizas, *I elliniki politiki meta ton Emfylio*, 453.

30 On this see Kostis Kornetis, *Children of the Dictatorship – Student Resistance, Cultural Politics and the "Long 1960s" in Greece* (New York: Berghahn, 2013).

31 For more information on this see Giorgos Voukelatos, *Quellenstraße 2 – Germania 1960-1974: agones kai paraskinia* [Quellenstraße 2 – Germany 1960-1974: Fight and Resistance] (Athens: Libro, 2003).

32 For more details see Kostas Nikolaou, *Ora Ellados: 21:40-22:40* [Greek Time: 21:40-22:40] (Athens: Kochlias, 1975), 12-13; and Nikos Papanastasiou, *Antistasi apo Mikrofonou – O Pavlos Mpakogiannis apenanti sti diktatoria ton syntagmatarchon* [Resistance via Microphone – Pavlos Bakojiannis against the Dictatorship of the Colonels] (Athens: Papadopoulos, 2020).

33 The *Deutsche Welle*, founded in 1953, was to "convey the new, democratic Germany and medially accompany its readmission to the international community". Deutsche Welle, 19 April 2013, *Drei Stunden via Kurzwelle*: http://www.dw.com/de/drei-stunden-via-kurzwelle-auf-deutsch/a-16684103 (last access 10 May 2022).

34 "We are going to influence the department for broadcasts in Greek language at the *Deutsche Welle* in this sense. Representatives and proponents of the current Greek regime should not be selected as candidates of the Federal Republic visitor programme and the invitation programme of the BPA." AAPD 24 August 1967, doc. no. 308, 1223.

35 Cf. Nikolaou, *Ora Ellados*, 26-7.

36 Cf. Voukelatos, *Quellenstraße 2*, 265.

37 "The majority of Greek migrant workers who opposed the junta lived in Germany. Criticism was voiced in Germany that hurt

the Colonels at home: millions of Greeks listened to the Greek department of the *Deutsche Welle* – just as millions of Germans listened to the BBC during the war – to the programmes of the *Bayerische Rundfunk* for Greek migrant workers and to the WDR evening TV shows for foreigners on Channel Three, influenced by the regime critics Pavlos Bakojannis and Basil Mathiopoulos". "Aufwand für Veröffentlichungen. Spiegel-Report über den Umgang der gestürzten Athener Obristen-Junta mit westdeutschen Journalisten," *Der Spiegel* 45/1976, 161–182.

38 In my doctoral thesis on Greek Migration to the Federal Republic, I discuss the surveillance of Greeks living in West Germany in greater detail.

39 "The perceptions of foreign countries are wrong. They are based on misinformation." General Pattalos insisted two weeks after the putsch in an interview with *Der Spiegel*. "Wir fanden aufgebohrte Jagdwaffen," *Der Spiegel* 21/1967, 113.

40 Alexis Kyrou was a diplomat with a Greek-Cyprian background and brother of the editor of the influential conservative daily *Hestia* in Greece. From 1947 to 1953 he was the Permanent Representative of Greece to the UN. One of his guiding principles was loyalty to NATO and the strengthening of relations with the USA. For more on Alexis Kyrou see Evanthis Hatzivassiliou, *Greece and the Cold War Front Line State, 1952–1967* (New York: Routledge, 2006), 21–3.

41 Ambassador Kyrou to Gerhard Bogner, 5 May 1967, Bayerisches Hauptstaatsarchiv [BayHStA], StK 19164.

42 On the relations between the Greek DW journalists and their West German superiors cf. Nikolaou, *Ora Ellados*, 28–56.

43 Cf. ibid., 33–35.

44 Danae Coulmas, "Welche Spur kann man als Ausländer überhaupt in einem fremden Land hinterlassen?," in: Sefa Inci Suvak and Justus Herrmann (eds.), *In Deutschland angekommen: Einwanderer erzählen ihre Geschichte 1955-heute* (Gütersloh: wissenmedia, 2008), 25.

45 Cf. Rizas, *I elliniki politiki meta ton Emfylio*, 475.

46 Cf. Apostolopoulos, *Die griechisch-deutschen Nachkriegsbeziehungen*, 313

47 Cf. Mogens Pelt, *Tying Greece to the West: US-West German-Greek Relations 1949–74* (Copenhagen: Museum Tusculanum, 2006), 93.

48 Cf. ibid., 90–1 and 169.

49 Apart from the recruitment agreement of 30 March 1960, there was also the Greek-West German cultural agreement of 17 May 1956 and the agreement on economic cooperation of 27 November 1958.

50 On this see also *Deutscher Bundestag*, 5. Wahlperiode, 165. Sitzung, Bonn 2 April 1968, 8659.

51 This point also includes the complex question of the Federal Republic's arms exports during the 1960s and 1970s. For more information on this see Dimitrios Gounaris, *Die Geschichte der sozialliberalen Rüstungsexportpolitik – Ein Instrument der deutschen Außenpolitik 1969–1982* (Wiesbaden: Springer, 2019).

52 For more information on Willy Brandt's foreign policy cf. Bernd Rother, *Willy Brandts Außenpolitik: Grundlagen, Methoden und Formen*, in: id. (ed.), *Willy Brandts Außenpolitik* (Wiesbaden: Springer, 2013), 335–358.

53 Cf. Philipp Rock, *Macht, Märkte und Moral*, (Frankfurt a. M.: Peter Lang, 2010), 78.

54 Cf. AAPD 24 August 1967, doc. no. 308, 1220.

55 Cf. Rock, *Macht*, 89.

56 Cf. AAPD 2 September 1969, doc. no. 276, 958–9.

57 AAPD, 24 August 1967, doc. no. 308, 1222.

58 Cf. AAPD 3 March 1970, doc. no. 86, 353. According to Rock, the threat of the military junta potentially leaning towards the Soviet Union was never serious and only intended to strengthen the Greek negotiation position. Cf. Rock, *Macht*, 90.

59 Cf. State Secretary Sackmann to Federal

59 Minister Heubl, 18 June 1969, BayHStA, StK 13173.
60 Cf. SPD press service, 26 March 1968, http://libraryfes.de/spdpd/1968/680326.pdf (last access 20 April 2022)
61 Willy Brandt, *My Life in Politics* (New York: Viking, 1992), 314.
62 Ibid., 450.
63 In the Bundestag debate on 13 October 1967, he mentioned the expatriation of the Greek actress and dissident Melina Merkouri, alluding to the methods of the "Third Reich". "It is well known that Greek citizens can lose their citizenship because of their oppositional stance towards their government. This has happened before elsewhere. There are some people here in the assembly hall who know how that is." *Deutscher Bundestag*, 5 Wahlperiode, 126. Sitzung, Bonn 13 October 1967, 6335 BC.
64 Cf. Mathiopoulos, *Willy Brandt*, 24–5.
65 Cf. Brandt, *My Life*, 314.
66 Cf. Rock, *Macht*, 103.
67 Cf. Referat I A 4 vol. 435, quoted in AAPD 19 April 1972, doc. no. 102, 423.
68 "Gauner- oder Gangsterstück?," *Die Zeit* 28 April 1972.
69 Cf. ibid., 58.
70 *Deutscher Bundestag*, 5. Wahlperiode, 126. Sitzung, Bonn 13 October 1967, 6335 BC.
71 Cf. Brandt, *Erinnerungen*, 347
72 Cf. "Bessere Demokraten," *Der Spiegel* 42/1969, 27; and State Secretary Sackmann to Federal Minister Heubl, 18 June 1969, BayHStA, StK 13173.
73 Cf. Rock, *Macht*, 68.
74 State Secretary Sackmann to Federal Minister Heubl, 18 June 1969, BayHStA, StK 13173.
75 Cf. ibid.
76 As early as shortly after the putsch, the CSU showed its willingness to support the military government when Franz Dannecker, CSU member of the Bundestag and a close friend of Franz Josef Strauß, informed the Greek embassy that he intended to meet with leading representatives of the new government in Greece. Cf. on this Ambassador Kyrou to the Greek Foreign Ministry 30 May 1967, Historical Archives of the Greek Ministry of Foreign Affairs, Athens.
77 "Bessere Demokraten," *Der Spiegel* 42/1969, 24.
78 The Foreign Office reacted displeased to Sackmann's trip and the remarks of the CSU leadership. According to Brandt's State Secretary Georg Ferdinand Duckwitz they provided a "threat to the well-balanced policy" of the Federal government. State Secretary Duckwitz to Federal Minister Heubl, 21 October 1969, BayHStA, StK 13173.
79 "Griechenland: Krücke für Chikre," *Der Spiegel* 39/1976, 138.
80 Cf. "Dummes Salz," *Der Spiegel* 33/1968, 19–21.
81 Cf. Attentismus in Griechenland, Bericht des Botschafters Onken aus Athen, 25 January 1974, BayHStA, StK 13173.
82 Cf. ibid.
83 Hagen Fleischer, *Krieg und Nachkrieg – Das schwierige deutsch-griechische Jahrhundert* (Cologne: Böhlau, 2020), 257.

Dimitrios K. Apostolopoulos

The German Federal Government vs. the Colonels 1967–1974: a Controversial Relationship

During the second half of the 20th century, the state of Greek-German relations improved rapidly. This was remarkable given the backdrop of World War II and especially the harsh German occupation of Greece, characterised by military retaliation measures, economic misery and famine.[1] The newly constituted Federal Republic of Germany sent one of its first six diplomatic representations to Athens at the end of 1950. This is indicative of the importance it attached to relations with Greece and to their normalisation. On the other hand, the Greek state, which was trying to stand on its own feet after having suffered a civil war in the wake of the Second World War and occupation, immediately showed good faith. All post-war Greek governments considered the new Federal Republic of Germany as radically differed from the 'Third Reich'.

Especially the accession of both countries to the Western Alliance – in times of Cold War – as well as the post-war economic interests that arose for both sides were beneficial for the bilateral relations. Athens put forward the argument of a *moral duty* due to the historical burden of the war and the occupation, for Bonn to provide generous financial aid and technical support for the exploitation of raw materials and the creation of an industrial and public infrastructure. As a counterbalance to the financial benefits Greece would receive for its post-war reconstruction, Germany would not only enjoy financial advantages (as the German industry, which was also going through a recovery phase, would gain from Greek reconstruction), but, above all, political benefits – meaning, at a bilateral level, a normalisation of relations by moving on from the past of war and occupation and, at the international level, the official Greek support of NATO's position on the German question.[2]

By the end of the 1950s, West Germany, as a member of NATO (since 1955) and one of the six founding members of the EEC (1957), already played a major role in the West. The close bilateral relations were at this point well established, since Bonn saw Athens as a "cornerstone of the free world" and "bastion against Communism",[3] and decisively supported Greece's efforts to become the first associated member of the EEC (which succeeded in 1961).[4] In this manner, context of the Cold War defined the relations between the two countries.

Concerned about Greece's place in the West, Bonn would keep a watchful eye on its internal political situation, especially when it seemed to destabilise in the mid-1960s.[5] In a memorandum dispatched at the end of 1966, the German ambassador in Athens, Oskar Schlitter, stressed the need to financially support the Greek government of Stefanos Stefanopoulos in order to stabilise the situation in Greece. He even noted prophetically that a potential fall of the government could lead to the imposition of a dictatorship:[6] [the support]

> "is a political decision concerning an allied friendly country at a nerve centre of world politics in Europe, where – due to the massive efforts of East-Germany to invade financially and politically – our vital interests are affected more than ever. On these grounds alone we should announce to the Greek government our intent for measures providing further financial aid in 1967."[7]

1967: The Federal Government in confusion

Although the West German ambassador to Greece closely observed the political anomalies of the period 1965–66, the imposition of the dictatorial regime in Athens left the government in Bonn perplexed. On the one hand, voices condemning the coup were also being heard inside Germany, and some countries proposed the interruption of diplomatic relations (especially the Scandinavian governments, which would later on also take the lead in the suspension or expulsion of Greece from the Council of Europe).[8] On the other hand, the Colonels' government did not essentially distance itself from the politics of the former Greek governments at an international level, and, rejecting East-German financial offers, showed the will to cooperate economically with the West only.[9]

In the first hours of the establishment of the April 21 regime, Greece's loyalty to its alliances was officially declared, a fact that calmed the western world in the first phase. In general, the foreign policy of the dictatorship remained steadfastly NATO-friendly and generally pro-Western throughout its seven years. From his viewpoint, the German ambassador in Athens recommended that his government adopt a moderate position towards the dictatorial regime and that it should avoid any behaviour that could cause changes to the political orientation of the military government. More precisely, a few days after the coup, in May 1967, he wrote in another memorandum:

> "The events of the 20th/21st April surely were a blow to the rule of law which partly took place under very bad conditions [...] On the other hand, it cannot be overlooked that the overt or covert effort to avoid the Communist threat is in principle positive for the Alliance and more specially for German interests".[10]

According to the ambassador, Bonn should aim at influencing the new military government with friendly advice, and in any case avoid any kind of pressure. Indeed, in Schlitter's analysis, a potential turn of Greece towards neutrality would have consequences for issues vital to Germany, as for example the German Issue, for policies towards Eastern Bloc countries and the relations of West Germany with the Arab states, as well as affecting German economic, political and cultural interests in Greece.[11]

Although Bonn chose to maintain diplomatic and economic contacts with the military regime in Athens, it nevertheless let it be known that Germany would adopt a 'wait-and-see' approach concerning the restitution of democracy in Greece. Many times – beginning in the first days of the dictatorship – it provided official support to ensure the freedom of Greek democrats. This was the case, for example, for the journalist Vassos Mathiopoulos, who was in Greece during the coup and whom the junta had decided to arrest. With the intervention of the German government, the German ambassador in Athens was called to grant asylum to Mathiopoulos, and to ensure he would be free to join his family in Germany.[12]

Moreover, the official declaration of the German minister of foreign affairs and social democratic party leader Willy Brandt before the Bundestag during the autumn of 1967, in which he stated that West-Germany was particularly worried about the events in Greece and wished for a quick return to democracy. This declaration mirrored the particular sensitivity of the Social Democratic Party (SPD) and marked the party's distinct approach within the federal government of the 'Grand Coalition' government (formed between Christian democrats and Social democrats).[13]

West-German society standing with Greek democrats/

While the federal government reacted with moderation to the imposition of a dictatorial regime in Greece, at the same time, it had to consider the reaction of the West German society, which expressed its support to Greek democrats from the very beginning. As early as in April 1967, the German Trade Union Confederation (DGB) requested the immediate restitution of democracy in Greece and the liberation of Greek prisoners. In a declaration, it pledged solidarity with the Greek people and especially the Greek workers and students in West-Germany.[14]

While official bilateral relations continued in the framework of financial agreements and the military cooperation inside NATO, it soon became clear that Bonn would have to take public opinion seriously into account. It was the government's intention that its intergovernmental contacts should receive only low-level press coverage in the two countries and, above all, that such contacts should not be reported as signs of an unreserved Greek-German collaboration. Even the Greek-language radio broadcasts of Deutsche Welle and the Munich radio station with Paylos Bakogiannis,[15] which were also listened to in Greece, were called on to clearly manifest the Federal Republic of Germany's wish for the restitution of democracy.[16]

One cannot ignore the fact that more than 200,000 Greek migrant workers and many more students had immigrated to West Germany, mostly recruited as *Gastarbeiter* ('guest workers') in the decade following the signature of a bilateral agreement on labour recruitment (30 March 1960).[17] This presence offered the possibility for closer contacts and interaction between the two populations, which during the dictatorship transformed into a joint struggle for the restitution of democracy in Greece.

The political activism of Greek citizens against the junta on German soil caused displeasure among the military government in Athens. The dictatorial regime repeatedly expressed its dissatisfaction to the Federal government at official level, especially concerning the Greek broadcasts on the German radio. Meanwhile it acknowledged that Bonn retained a more moderate stance than other Western governments.[18]

The Colonels' dictatorship in the international context

As mentioned, throughout the dictatorship, Greece's international policy orientation towards the West remained stable. This formal commitment of the Colonels from as early as April 1967 caused US Secretary of State Dean Rusk – despite the first confusion of the State Department, since both the US ambassador and the head of the CIA in Athens did not initially know the leaders of the coup – to express his relative satisfaction with the pro-Atlantic stance of the dictatorial leadership. Rusk also noted, however, that American cooperation would hinge on progress towards the restoration of constitutional freedoms, without this being demanded immediately, but as soon as possible. The American side wanted, on the one hand, to see the king regain his leadership and impose his authority on the junta. On the other, it maintained a controversial stance on the military regime, struggling to reconcile its military and economic interests in the region with democratic sensitivities – under pressure from both domestic and international public opinion.[19]

The outbreak of the Arab-Israeli war in June 1967, however, prompted American policy to abandon, at the declarative level, the calls for a restoration of democracy in Greece and, in essence, to show a friendly or at least more-than-tolerant attitude towards the dictatorship of the Colonels. During the Six Day War, the junta seemed particularly cooperative, allowing the unimpeded use of US facilities on Greek soil. Greece remained pro-American at a time when the Soviet Union's presence and influence in the Mediterranean was growing, and the US therefore saw it as necessary to secure the American position and facilities on Greek territory. A letter from President Johnson in early 1968 completely restored contacts between the United States and the military regime in Athens.[20]

Certainly, US-Greek relations were not entirely uneventful over the seven years as the US governments had to take into account American public opinion and especially the reactions of congressional liberals, as for example Senator Fulbright. Yet even the military regime in Greece could not ignore internal voices by several military government officials opposed to the warm embrace with the US. Any entanglements in the relations between the two countries in the period 1967–74 had more to do with tactical maneuvers of their respective governments or with movements of internal balance than with genuine bilateral problems. In fact, nothing could undermine the pro-American orientation of the military regime or the pro-regime stance of the United States, either during the Johnson administration until the beginning of 1969 or during Nixon's term (January 1969 – August 1974).[21]

As for the dictatorship's relations with Europe's hard core, the relations continued in about the same pattern. Except for the freeze of the 1961 Association Agreement between Greece and the EEC, which was not a difficult decision since it did not harm the interests of the six Member States, there was no interruption of commercial, investment or military relations with the Junta.[22] Even in the period before the dictatorship, its domestic political situation did not allow Greece to make the drastic adjustments to its administrative mechanisms and economic structures required in order to gradually achieve the integration of the Greek economy into the European one envisaged in the 1961 Association Agreement. During the seven years of dictatorship, only the obligations of the Greek side, related to the customs union were implemented, and no adjustment of institutions was prepared to set the ground for full integration. Financial assistance from the EEC was 'frozen' in 1967. In fact, out of the total of $ 125 m of the European Investment Bank, only $ 55 m were absorbed by the end of the seven years.[23]

Contrary to the EEC-members' reaction towards the Colonels, the Scandinavian governments were more active against the junta since 1967. Indeed, Denmark, Norway and Sweden immediately tried to isolate the Greek dictatorial regime in two international fora: NATO and the Council of Europe. In NATO, the attempt failed as, in a tense international environment, strategic interests of the Alliance members prevailed over democratic values and the rule of law. The Council of Europe, on the other hand, offered more fertile ground for such efforts. The Nordic countries and the Netherlands already filed actions on 20 and 27 September 1967, seeking the expulsion of Greece for violating a number of fundamental rights guaranteed in the European Convention on Human Rights.[24]

In 1968, the question of how to act towards the junta, which had a negative image among the Western coalition because it had resolved the Parliament, banned the political parties and arrested numerous politicians – especially from the left wing and centre party – was urgently raised on a European political level. It was obvious that the regime was violating human rights by: a legal state of siege in peace times, imposing exile, suspending regular trials, establishing concentration camps, imprisoning resistance fighters and prosecuting citizens in special military courts. It was against this backdrop that a lawsuit was filed at the European Court of Human Rights (ECHR) in Strasbourg and the expulsion of the Athens regime from the Council of Europe was requested.[25]

Finally, in December 1969 – under pressure mainly from the Nordics, but also from other countries – Greece withdrew from the Council of Europe, in order to prevent its condemnation for human rights violations. This process, launched in the beginning of 1969 on the initiative of the Dutch representative Max van der Stoel, was essentially an expulsion from an institution that acted as the guardian of the values of the Western world. It went ahead despite a behind-the-scenes American effort to avert the condemnation of Athens, aiming to prevent an isolation of the regime which it viewed as detrimental to the Atlantic Alliance, given that most members of the Council were also NATO members.[26]

The French side also stressed the need to prevent an isolation of Greece from its allies. In fact, in the period of 1972–74 Paris became the second largest supplier of weapons systems to the Greek armed forces, after the USA. Generally, despite the fact that the dictatorship was incompatible with the post-war historical condemnation of fascism and authoritarianism, Western European countries acted pragmatically in their relations with the military regime. Several governments thus saw the Council of Europe case as an opportunity to condemn the junta, so that they would not have to take other measures in their bilateral relations with Athens.

The Greek case in the Council of Europe put Bonn in a difficult position. The question of the German stance within the Council of Europe was raised in a cabinet meeting of the German government at the end of 1968. All agreed that the exclusion of Greece from the Council of Europe could make up for the avoidance of measures at the bilateral level. The expulsion would not be directed at the nation, but rather against the military regime which had not been elected by the people. The Statute of the Council of Europe indeed provided that only democracies could become members.[27] Thus, the only powerful intervention of Europe (and West Germany) against the Colonels took place at the Council of Europe.

The fact that Greece was forced to withdraw from the Council of Europe in December 1969 to avoid its condemnation for human rights violations, combined with Willy Brandt's becoming Chancellor in October of the same year, created new circumstances in the relations of the dictatorial regime with the Western governments, including West Germany. In fact, leaks from the military government in Athens revealed that it was the position of West Germany and of Brandt personally – since, at the last moment, he supported the Scandinavian governments' stance[28] – that determined the fate of Greece in the Council of Europe.

Early on, the head of the Social democratic party took a stand concerning the dictatorial regime, not only in his speeches before the Bundestag. In his previous position as vice chancellor and minister of foreign affairs of the 'grand coalition', he refused to get off the plane at a stopover at the Athens airport on his return from an official visit to Turkey, in order to demonstrate his opposition to the political situation in Greece. Furthermore, he agreed to meet politicians like Andreas Papandreou in order to make Germany's recognition of political opponents to the dictatorship officially known. There is no doubt that politicians like Willy Brandt contributed to a relative isolation of the regime and to the moral and financial support of the activists for the restitution of democracy.

Difficult balance in bilateral relations

From 1969 on, the bilateral relations became perceptibly more difficult, not just concerning Greece in the Council of Europe. In addition to the purely political matter and the question of recognition or non-recognition of the Greek government, the German treatment of individual Greek democrats is also worth mentioning. The moral support and solidarity, as well as the practical help to hundreds of thousands of Greek workers, students and researchers in Germany are undeniable. This was especially true considering that many Greeks had requested and been granted asylum in Germany.

During this period, the West German government was in a very challenging position since it tried to find the balance between, on the one hand, securing its economic and political interests in Greece and, on the other hand, ideologically and morally supporting the fight of Greek citizens and politicians for the restitution of democracy. The latter was unconditionally defended by the parliamentary group of the Social democratic party inside the government as well as the majority of West German society.

Consequently, the Colonels' position towards the West German government became more cautious. From 1970 until the fall of the dictatorship, the German government as well as the political parties officially condemned the dictatorial regime and called for the restitution of democracy in Greece. The German industry however took a more ambiguous stance in order to maintain its existing economic relations with the junta.[29]

In fact, diplomatic relations of the two countries were often balanced on the razor's edge, also because of the repeated meetings of the German ambassador in Athens, Peter Limbourg, with Greek opposition politicians. Indeed, he was declared a *persona non grata* by the junta in spring 1972 and was ultimately recalled by Bonn in response to the notorious case of Professor Georg Alexandros Mangakis.[30] At the same period, efforts by the West German and other governments contributed to the non-execution of a special military court sentence condemning Alekos Panagoulis to death.[31]

Beyond the evident political and moral support from Germany, there was also material assistance. Indeed, an employee of the German embassy in Athens was specifically tasked with helping families of imprisoned or exiled activists on various islands. Moreover, the whole German support at an official level was enhanced by cultural institutions and the media. Goethe-Institut, German radio stations, the German press and, above all, the Greek-language broadcasts of Deutsche Welle and Bayerischer Rundfunk unreservedly supported the restitution of democracy in Greece and at the same time facilitated the federal government's efforts to great degree.

This did not mean that Willy Brandt, as chancellor, had not realised that he had to safeguard German interests at a time when the Nixon administration had abandoned any pretexts from the beginning of 1969 and accepted the dictatorship as a *fait accompli*. This attitude was due to the perception that the dictatorship, desirable or not, was identified with NATO and the Western world, which meant that Greece would remain an ally of the West in the Cold War. Especially after Richard Nixon took power, with Henry Kissinger as his national security adviser, Washington's primary goal became to reaffirm the US strategic presence in the world by strengthening pro-US regimes, regardless of their political nature.

Moreover, Washington, in contrast to the Western European governments, argued that there was no active opposition to the regime and its methods among the Greek population that would justify

American pressure for democratization.[32] Obviously, this attitude of the US government directly affected West German foreign policy.

Finally, Greek-German diplomatic relations were not officially severed and the junta government was formally recognised, a decision facilitated by the preservation of the monarchy until 1973. At the official level, Bonn may have held a wait-and-see attitude towards the military regime but it should be noted that official visits by members of the federal government to Greece were avoided during those seven years, and, of course, no minister of the regime was formally admitted to Germany.[33]

Conclusion

In conclusion, during the seven years from 1967–1974, relations between Athens and its Western Allies took place on two levels. On the one hand, in the case of the United States of America, *realpolitik* had absolute dominance in relations with the junta, especially after Nixon took over the presidency. The Americans accepted the military regime and finally came to the perception that the dictatorship did not constitute such a fundamental deviation from democracy in Greece, which anyhow had been replaced by authoritarian regimes in the past.

Suggestions for regime liberalisation remained at an abstract level, and the main goal of the US was to secure its strategic interests in the sensitive region of the Eastern Mediterranean.

On the other hand, for Western Europe the dictatorship in Greece was not an acceptable regime in terms of democratic values, although the Colonels had initially met a wider international tolerance for about two years. Most Western European democracies – with some exceptions mainly from the Scandinavian countries – wanted to respect the principle of non-interference in 'Greek internal affairs'. However, the Europeans' opposition to the military regime was visible, mainly in the Colonels' relations with the Council of Europe and secondarily within the EEC.

Opposition to the junta was expressed in a wide range of countries and political parties. The socialist parties in particular were more critical than the conservatives, but this did not mean that they could steer Western European governments away from a *realpolitik* dictated by the need for Greek participation in NATO in the Cold War.

In this context, West Germany followed a moderate policy towards the Colonels' dictatorship in Greece, similar to those of the US and its main European partners, considering that the survival of the regime would secure German interests. The federal government's main argument for not taking official action against the regime was to not jeopardise the cohesion of the North Atlantic Alliance in its south-eastern wing, which was nearer to the unstable Middle East. Furthermore, the whole attitude of Bonn could also be explained by the complete alignment of West-Germany's foreign policy with US foreign policy. The United States worked in order not to isolate the regime, an action which would damage the Atlantic Alliance.

At a political and communication level, a turning point of Bonn-Athens relations during the seven years of dictatorship can be seen at the moment of the assumption of the Chancellorship by Willy Brandt in autumn 1969. The historical tragedy Germany had been through had taught it essential lessons. The Nazi dictatorship had lasted 12 years (1933–45) and had spelled disaster for the whole world and also for Germany. Hence it was only logical that the German democrats would not remain indifferent to the political divergence which was happening to another European country.

At a societal level, there were many moral and practical manifestations of solidarity towards the Greek democrats in Germany, as well as in other European countries. Especially after 1969, the German federal government ensured that the junta leadership was aware that their violent repression did not pass unnoticed by the eyes of the world.

The period of 1967–74 reshaped Greek-German relations. Although officially the trauma of World War II had been mostly healed through political negotiations, financial agreements and political visits at a governmental level, it was this seven-year period that actually gave both sides a historical opportunity for rapprochement both at a societal and individual level, which would go on to have a positive impact on the broader political and financial relations between the two states in the future.

1. About the German occupation in Greece and the retaliation measures, see Hagen Fleischer, "Die deutsche Militärverwaltung in Griechenland [The German military administration in Greece]," in *Die Bürokratie der Okkupation. Strukturen der Herrschaft und Verwaltung im besetzten Europa [The bureaucracy of the occupation. Structures of power and administration in occupied Europe]*, ed. Wolfgang Benz, Johannes Houwink ten Cate, Gerhard Otto (Berlin: Metropol, 1998), 65 ff.

2. About post-war Greek-German relations, see Dimitrios Apostolopoulos, *Die griechisch-deutschen Nachkriegsbeziehungen, historische Hypothek und moralischer Kredit: Die bilateralen politischen und ökonomischen Beziehungen unter besonderer Berücksichtigung des Zeitraums 1958-67 [Post-War Greek-German Relations, Historical Burden and Moral Credit: The bilateral political and economic relations with special reference to the period 1958-67]* (Frankfurt a. M.: Peter Lang, 2004).

3. The quotations belong to Konrad Adenauer, the first chancellor of West Germany. This is how he characterised Greece in an interview with the newspaper Kathimerini, during his official visit to the country in March 1954 – the first official visit of a German head of government since the founding of the modern state of Greece in 1830-32. Griechenland: Eckpfeiler der freien Welt [Greece: Cornerstone of the free world], in: *Kathimerini*, 10 March 1954, Bulletin des Presse- und Informationsamtes der Bundesregierung, März 1954/Nr. 47, 377.

4. Alfred Müller-Armack (Secretary of State, Federal Ministry of Economics), Die Assoziation Griechenlands mit der EWG aus deutscher Sicht [The association of Greece with the EEC from a German point of view], Politisches Archiv des Auswärtigen Amtes [PA AA], Ref. 206, Bd. 127.

5. Fernschreiben Nr. 364 des Botschafters Schlitter [Tele-type Report of the German Ambassador in Athens], 26 September 1965, in: *Akten zur Auswärtigen Politik der Bundesrepublik Deutschland 1965, Vol. III*, 366.

6. Zusammenstellung der wichtigsten Daten für Griechenland nach dem Stand vom 1. Januar 1966 [Summary of the Most Important Data for Greece as of January 1, 1966], PA AA, Ref. I A 4, Bd. 328.

7. Fernschreiben Nr. 77 des Botschafters Schlitter [Tele-type Report of the German Ambassador in Athens], 24 March 1966, in: *Akten zur Auswärtigen Politik der Bundesrepublik Deutschland 1966, Vol. I*, 363 f.

8. Sprechzettel, Betreff: Haltung der Bundesregierung zum derzeitigen griechischen Regime, unter Berücksichtigung des Auftrags der Fraktion der SPD [Speaker's note, regarding: The Attitude of the Federal Government to the Current Greek Regime, Taking into Account the Mandate of the SPD Parliamentary Group], PA AA, Ref. I A 4, Bd. 412.

9. Pantelis Giakoumis, *Zwischen den Fronten: Die Sicherheitspolitik Griechenlands [Between the fronts: Greece's Security Policy]* (Münster: Lit, 1987), 102.

10. Aufzeichnung des Botschafters Schlitter, Betreff: Griechenland; hier: Analyse der Lage nach dem Militärputsch vom

10 20./21. April 1967 [Note by Ambassador Schlitter, regarding: Greece; here: Analysis of the situation after the military coup of April 20/21, 1967], 26 May 1967, PA AA, Bestand B 150.
11 Note by Ambassador Schlitter, 1967, ibid.
12 Willy Brandt, *Mia zoi agones* [*A lifetime of battles*], ed. Vasos Mathiopoulos (Athens: Dimosiografikos Organismos Lambraki, 1989), 34.
13 Mitteilung an die Presse, Nr. 1502/67 veröffentlicht durch das Presse- und Informationsamt der Bundesregierung [Press Release, No. 1502/67, published by the Press and Information Office of the Federal Government], 13 October 1967, PA AA, Ref. I A 4, Bd. 415.
14 Airgram from the American Embassy in Athens to the Department of State, West German Trade Union Opposition to the Military Regime in Greece, 8 May 1967, National Archives and Records Administration [NARA], RG 59, Political Aff. & Rel. Gerw-G; see also *Handelsblatt*, 26 April 1967.
15 For the Bavarian radio broadcasts and Paylos Bakogiannis, see Nikos Papanastasiou, *Antistasi apo mikrofonou: O Paylos Bakogiannis apenanti sti diktatoria ton syntagmatarchon* [*Resistance from a microphone. Paylos Bakogiannis against the dictatorship of the colonels*] (Athens: Papadopoulos Publications, 2020).
16 Airgram (Confidential) from the American Embassy in Athens to the Department of State, German Embassy's Relations with Greek Government, 1 February 1968, NARA, RG 59, Political Aff. & Rel. Gerw-G and Fernschreiben (geheim) vom Staatssekretär Duckwitz an den Botschafter in Athen persönlich [Telex (secret) from the German State Secretary Duckwitz to the Federal Government's Ambassador in Athens personally], 16 January 1968, PA AA, Bestand B 150.
17 Text of the Agreement, PA AA, Ref. 206, Bd. 127.
18 Politischer Jahresbericht 1967 [Annual Political Report 1967], PA AA, Ref. I A 4, Bd. 411.
19 Sotiris Rizas, *I Elliniki Politiki meta ton Emfylio Polemo. Koinovouleytismos kai Diktatoria* [*Greek Politics after the Civil War. Parliamentarism and Dictatorship*] (Athens: Kastaniotis Publications, 2008), 429 ff.
20 Ibid.
21 The issue of US involvement in the 1967 coup has been and still is an object of theories and study. Washington's positive attitude towards the junta has raised suspicions among the Greek public about the role of the United States in supporting the April regime. According to rumors, some role was played by American intelligence officials, with whom Papadopoulos was apparently in contact – without perhaps the direct involvement of the US embassy in Athens. However, the real relationship of both Papadopoulos and later Ioannidis with these services has not been verified. See, among others, Konstantinos Tsoukalas, *I elliniki tragodia* [*The Greek Tragedy*] (Athens: Patakis Publications, 2020); Andreas Papandreou, *Democracy at Gunpoint* (Wien: Molden, 1971); Alexis Papachelas, *O viasmos tis ellinikis dimokratias* [*The rape of the Greek Republic*] (Athens: Estia, 2017); Theodore Couloumbis, *The United States, Greece and Turkey. The troubled triangle* (New York: Praeger, 1983).
22 Arne Treholt, "Europe and the Greek Dictatorship," in: *Greece under Military Rule*, ed. Richard Clogg and George Yannopoulos (London: Secker & Warburg, 1972), 225.
23 Rizas, *I Elliniki Politiki meta ton Emfylio Polemo*, 459.
24 James Becket, "The Greek Case before the European Human Rights Commission," in: *Human Rights* 1, no. 1 (August 1970), 94.
25 Christos Christidis, "I Eyropi enanti tis diktatorias ton syntagmatarchon: I periptosi tis ellinikis ypothesis sto Symvoulio tis Eyropis," in: *I diktatoria ton syntagmatarchon kai I apokatastasi tis dimokratias, Idryma tis Voulis ton Ellinon* ["Europe against the Dictator-

ship of the Colonels: the case of the Greek case in the Council of Europe," in: *The dictatorship of the colonels & the restoration of democracy, Conference Proceedings*], Foundation of the Greek Parliament for Parliamentarism and Democracy, 20–22 November 2014, 409–410.

26 Dimitris Konstas, *I Elliniki Ypothesi sto Symvoulio tis Evropis 1967–1969: Theoria kai praktiki politikis pieseos apo Diethneis Organismous* [*The Greek Case in the Council of Europe 1967–1969: Theory and practice of political pressure by International Organizations*] (Athens: Papazisis Publications, 1976), 103–104.

27 Brandt, *Mia zoi agones,* 28 f.

28 *The Times*, 12 December 1969.

29 Erwin Erasmus Koch, *Griechenland im Umbruch: Der NATO-Partner im Südosten* (Frankfurt a. M.: Maindruck, 1970), 13; Hagen Fleischer, "Vom Kalten Krieg zur 'Neuen Ordnung': Der Faktor Griechenland in der deutschen Außenpolitik [From the Cold War to the 'New Order': The Greek factor in German foreign policy]," *Thetis*, Bd. 3, (Mannheim: Harrassowitz, 1996), 305.

30 Mangakis was a visiting professor at the University of Freiburg in Germany before being appointed as a full professor at the School of Law at Athens University. In February 1969, Mangakis had been expelled from his position and was later on arrested for anti-dictatorial activities. He spent five months in solitary confinement, was tortured and condemned to 18 years in prison by a special court martial in April 1970. While he was incarcerated, the University of Heidelberg appointed him as professor for Penal Law and Philosophy of Law in 1972. In April of the same year, he was released from prison on health grounds. Many German friends of Mangakis' and especially Horst Ehmke, professor of constitutional law and member of Willy Brandt's cabinet, worried that he would be in constant danger while in Greece. They decided to bring him to Germany, facilitated by German and US-American ambassadors. A German Air Force aircraft was used to evacuate him, picking him up from the US base at Athens's Airport. Mangakis remained in Heidelberg for the next two years and continued his anti-dictatorial fight. See *Frankfurter Allgemeine Zeitung,* 19 April 1972; *Die Welt,* 19 April 1972; *Süddeutsche Zeitung,* 19 April 1972; *The Times-London,* 19 April 1972; *Le Monde,* 20 April 1972; *Die Welt,* 21 April 1972; *Neue Zürcher Zeitung,* 21 April 1972; *Der Spiegel,* 5 August 1985.

31 Brandt, *Mia zoi agone,* 34 f.

32 Rizas, *I Elliniki Politiki meta ton Emfylio Polemo,* 452 ff.

33 A. G. Xydis, "The Military Regime's Foreign Policy,": *Greece under Military Rule*, ed. Richard Clogg and George Yannopoulos (London: Secker & Warburg, 1972), 198.

Nikos Papanastasiou

Solidarity and Realpolitik? Chancellor Willy Brandt, the Colonels in Greece and the Dictatorships of the South

The Colonels' dictatorship in Greece (1967–74) became a critical test for the development of bilateral relations between Greece and the Federal Republic of Germany (FRG) that had been based for decades on close economic ties and was further facilitated by the constant increase of post-war Greek immigration to Germany in the 1960s. This posed a new challenge for German diplomacy, which even before the coup had predicted the establishment of a dictatorial regime. According to the West German Ambassador in Athens, Dr Oskar Schlitter, after 1967, Germany had to face the attempts by its Western partners and the Communist German Democratic Republic (GDR) for economic and political competition in Greece. Bonn opted for a cautious approach towards the Greek dictatorship and with no interruption of diplomatic relations in order not to undermine German interests in Greece. This approach finally prevailed within the coalition government in which Willy Brandt participated as Foreign Minister, without being influenced by the rhetoric of the Greek military dictatorship like other conservative politicians in Germany. The junta's rhetoric tried to portray the acts of the colonels as preventing measures to restore democracy, fight communism and to reinforce the fight against corruption and nepotism.[1]

Given that Brandt's life story was characterized by his struggle against Nazism and the dictatorships of the Iberian peninsula, his political action is still primarily identified with his effort to internationally isolate the dictatorship of the Colonels in Greece, supporting morally as well as practically the Greek resistance organizations. But one also has to analyse whether Brandt's approach towards Greece as the German Foreign Minister (1966–1969) and Chancellor (1969–1974) can be described as an attempt to strike a balance between solidarity with the opposition to the Greek Junta and a "realistic" approach to the dictatorial change in Greece, so as not to break economic ties with the junta regime. Did we have in the case of Greece under the Colonels a variation of Brandt's policy *Wandel durch Annäherung* – change through rapprochement – which is generally associated with Brandt's Ostpolitik, but was also implemented in his approach towards Spain and Portugal in the '60s?[2] At that time the Social Democrats abandoned the attempt to isolate of Franco's regime in order to allow Spain to come closer to Europe (through the prospect of becoming an associated member of the European Economic Community EEC), while Brandt as Foreign Minister did not make major changes to the Adenauer era policy towards Lisbon, as he remained convinced that close contacts would inevitably strengthen the prospect of Portugal moving towards democracy. This cautious approach towards the dictatorships on the Iberian Peninsula made the SPD's relations with the socialist opposition in those countries more complex. This was later expressed by leaders such as Mario Soares and Felipe Gonzalez[3] in their careful criticism of the attitude of the German Social Democrats.

Contacts between the German Social Democrats and Greek politicians and party officials – some of whom were even active in West Germany – can be dated back to the early 1960s, but links became closer after 1967 and the establishment of the Greek Military Dictatorship. SPD officials and especially the unions they were associated with supported the establishment of a Greek Centre Union party organisation in Germany (Bad Godesberg) under George Voukelatos, in the hope that all Centre Union Party members located in Western

Germany would later play a key role in re-establishing the party in Greece, based on the principles of European Social Democracy.[4]

During the Greek dictatorship, friendly relations developed between SDP executives and associates of opposition figure Andreas Papandreou. For instance, in difficult times of economic misery the prominent journalist Basil Mathiopoulos received financial support from his German comrades to promote his book *Sozialismus und soziale Frage in Griechenland* (Socialism and Social Issues in Greece) among SPD party members. Mathiopoulos then wanted to establish a newspaper for Greek immigrants to Germany after 1967, financed by the German government because he considered the relevant publication of the Federal Press Office (*Bundespresseamt*), *I Elliniki,* did not cover the needs of immigrants. However, his proposal was rejected as the German Ministry of Foreign Affairs feared the negative reaction of the colonels in Greece if they were to entrust this publication to an ardent government opponent such as Mathiopoulos. The SPD covered the living expenses of anti-dictatorial activists at that time, while also helping to approve applications for political asylum. That was the case of Akis Tsochatzopoulos who was the head of PAK-office (Panhellenic Liberation Front/PAK) in Munich and from 1967 a key member of the Committee for Democracy for Greece which was an initiative of the local SPD organisation in Munich.[5]

Before 1967, German Social democracy lacked a reliable partner among Greek politicians, many of whom fled Greece and established their political activity abroad after the establishment of the dictatorship. The most prominent case is that of Andreas Papandreou, who chose Sweden as the seat of the PAK. Although he had organisational support from the SPD to make West Germany the centre of his political activities, he kept his distance from the German Social Democrats. The fact that he was the representative of the Greek Centre Union abroad (the most dominant party in Greece prior to the coup), did not make it easier for SPD members to overcome their distrust towards Papandreou and his extreme anti-Western rhetoric. It was due to this tendency that the SPD did not recognise Papandreou and the Centre Union as sole representatives of Socialism in Greece.⁶

The gap between the SPD and Papandreou was reflected in the close relations that had developed with Giorgos Mavros, who founded the party Centre Union-New Forces, after 1974. Veronika Isenberg, a member of the SPD Bundestag fraction's Foreign Policy Working Group, expressed caution and asked Willy Brandt to keep the SPD's neutral stance towards the Greek political parties, and take the potential of the newly founded PASOK party (Panhellenic Socialist Movement) into account. She did not want to create the impression of external involvement in the first national elections after the restoration of democracy set for November, 17, 1974. Isenberg concluded that the SPD had genuine friends both in the centre-left party of G. Mavros and in the Social Democratic Party of Giorgos Alexandros Mangakis – Christos Protopapas, as well as in Papandreou's PASOK.⁷ The bad relationship with Papandreou poisoned the relations of the SPD with PASOK after the restoration of democracy in Greece to the extent that Helmut Schmidt saw Andreas Papandreou, the leader of the newly founded PASOK, as a populist in favour of the exit of Greece from NATO and against its joining the European Economic Community.⁸ In contrast, and despite the great distrust with which the socialist leaders in Spain and Portugal were treated by Brandt and the German Social Democrats for a long time, it can be seen that these contacts and organisational support played a role in consolidating the socialist parties as a serious alternative towards the restoration of democracy in these countries.⁹

German Vice Chancellor and Foreign Minister Willy Brandt was the centre of bilateral Greek-German relations after 1967. As a symbol for the relentless struggle against dictatorship, all opponents of the junta and the anti-dictatorial front in Greece and Germany placed high hopes on him. His intervention with the colonels for the release Basil Mathiopoulos, the most well-known Greek media representative in Germany who had been arrested together with a German TV crew in Athens, seemed to confirm the expectations that were placed on his shoulders.[10]

Immediately after the establishment of a military dictatorship in Greece, Brandt had already differentiated himself from many members of the federal government who were known for their timid approach towards the Greek military dictatorship. At that time Brand was trying to secure his party's confidence by considering the overriding preferences of West German public opinion and the trade unions for a critical stance against the Greek junta. Brandt even expressed the desire of the federal government for a swift restoration of democracy in Greece in a statement before the German Parliament: "We are particularly concerned about the violation of fundamental rights and the abolition of democracy in Greece" (October 13, 1967).[11] At the same time, he stressed the federal government's concern for "humanity, the rule of law and democracy, but also the credibility of organisations (such as NATO and the Council of Europe) of which we are members". Beyond the visionary side of Brandt, however, there was a pragmatist side, as reflected in his decision to set clear criteria for legal aid and other assistance to the regime's political prisoners since 1967, such as the possible connection with German nationals, studies in Germany, work experience as a migrant worker, or immediate danger to the life of a political prisoner.[12]

Whilst the *grand coalition* government[13] was in power in West Germany (1966–1969), the case of the Greek junta began to cause considerable turmoil among the government partners. At the same time, Brandt's approach highlighted differences in the Greek junta's treatment of the conservative camp, which, as in the case of Spain, regarded a stable dictatorial regime as the first step in a long road towards democratisation.

There were members of the federal cabinet such as Franz Josef Strauss, (minister of the treasury) and long-time Chairman of the CSU in Bavaria, who belonged to the loyal lobbyists of the colonels demanding the relaxation of the sanctions imposed by the European Economic Community (EEC) on Greece after the coup.[14] Strauss based his approach on the logic of exceptionalism, as Alexander Clarkson has put it. This approach of exceptionalism could be applied to relations with the Greek Junta as well as other authoritarian regimes such as Francoist Spain or various Turkish military governments. This argument was based on the idea that specific cultural factors in Mediterranean or the Balkan states barred the development of 'stable' (ie anti-communist) democracy, necessitating authoritarian forms of government.[15]

Although many believed that the two major German camps had reached a consensus on their policy towards the dictatorships in Spain (after 1964) and in the case of Portugal which was fighting a colonial war, Brandt was able to highlight that his attitude towards the dictatorships differed from that of the Christian Democrat conservatives. Contrary to the SPD, the Christian Democrats had few contacts with centre-right politicians in Greece before 1974. The CDU was not interested in entering into relations with the old political guard in Greece that belonged to the centre right, apart from the fact that there was no element of international solidarity that characterised the socialist parties.[16] On the other hand the SPD seemed determined to strengthen civil society and the socialist opposition in order to consolidate democracy in the long run in all three dictatorships of Europe's South, although in the case of the Iberian Peninsula these contacts became formal with the involvement of the Friedrich Ebert Foundation (a think tank associated with – but independent from – the SPD).[17]

After the abolition of a *cordon sanitaire* that the European Left and the SPD had drawn around the Franco regime from the 1940s into the mid-1960s, there appeared to be no qualms in early 1968 when four SPD MPs met with the Deputy Prime Minister of the Greek Junta, Pattakos, in Athens. Adolf Arndt, Hans Apel, Walter Faller, and Kurt Mattick were commissioned by the presidency of their party to assess the situation in Greece on the ground. When asked about the refusal of the regime to end the state of siege, Pattakos expressed anger about what he saw as an interference in the internal affairs of Greece and an attempt by Bonn "to create a second (Greek) Vietnam".[18] However, as the MPs wanted to show solidarity with political prisoners, they also visited the island of Leros on the Dodecanese archipelago, location of a prison camp which on their return to Germany, they described as a "European problem".[19]

After the restoration of democracy in Greece it was revealed that a British public relations company covered the expenses of holidays in Greece on behalf of the colonels for six French, eleven British and six MPs for the German parliament. It should be appreciated that none of the six German MPs were from the SPD, arguably thanks to its close ties with Greek resistance circles in Germany.[20]

After the return of the German MPs to Germany, Brandt stated that he was giving priority to *raison d'état* in an early attempt to reduce pressure from his party members for close bilateral ties with the junta. He was quoted by *Der Spiegel* as stating: "In the new foreign policy of the federal government free of ideological barriers, diplomatic relations have nothing to do with the approval of this regime". He also stated that "anyone who pushes for the severance of diplomatic relations with Athens ignores the interests [of the FRG]". He believed that a hardening of attitudes towards Athens would serve Bonn's rivals – France, Britain and the Soviet bloc. It became increasingly clear that even the social democratic forces in the major western countries, which had traditionally placed more emphasis on the protection of human rights and maintained close ties with Greek resistance circles, intended to exercise *realpolitik* towards the Greek junta.[21]

The implementation of the SPD's election manifesto in the September 1969 elections for "more democracy" (*Wir wollen mehr Demokratie wagen*) did not mean that the Brandt government would adopt the foreign policy framework favoured by the Scandinavian countries since it would inevitably lead to a clash with colonels. The Social Democrat chancellor himself, it seemed, was fully aware of the fact that in order to defend German interests in Greece in the context of (economic) competition from Western powers, he could not avoid actions that would legitimise the rule of the junta regime.[22]

The fact that Germany opted for the suspension of Greece's participation in the Council of Europe instead of its expulsion must be seen as an act of delicate balance with the internal party opposition and international partners and even towards the colonels in Greece. German policy rapprochement towards Athens after 1970 – at a time when the colonels' regime was advertising its liberalisation – led to the delivery of German military equipment to Greece in the form of NATO aid and also to the construction of Greek submarines in German shipyards which had been ordered in 1967.[23]

This helped the bilateral relations gradually gain momentum and even allowed a visit of the German Deputy Foreign Minister, Paul Frank, to Greece in September 1972. Although the new social-liberal coalition (between the SPD and the Free Democratic Party FDP) was criticised by the press for "misapplied German realpolitik" towards Greece, this attitude was more an attempt to prevent permanent damage to Germany from the 'Mangakis case' by restarting Greek-German relations in the years of Brandt chancellery.[24] Germany's influence and its involvement in Spain and Portugal were much bigger than in Greece. This influence gained a new quality when the SPD developed ties with several Spanish and Portuguese socialist politicians in the Brandt years that eventually paid off for both sides during the transition to democracy. It is well known that Brandt supported close relations between the EEC and Spain as an associated member, as he considered that close bilateral relations promoted modernisation to an extent that would allow democracy to emerge after Franco's death.

As head of the SPD, Willy Brandt initiated a notable measure of flexibility towards the dictatorships of Spain and Portugal in the 1960s that was to be continued in the years of the grand coalition (1966–1969) and later during his chancellery, so as to bridge the gap with democratic Europe.[25] In the case of Greece during the Colonels' regime, Brandt felt from the start that he had to combine the demand for democratisation in Greece with *raison d'état* as he considered his approach towards Spain and Portugal overall very successful and mutually beneficial.

The obvious differences in Brandt's approach to the democratic and anti-dictatorial forces in the 1970s on the Iberian Peninsula and in Greece go back to the fact Brandt was a leading figure in German Politics (Foreign Minister and later chancellor until May 1974) throughout the Colonels dictatorship. As Dr. Bernd Rother put it, Brandt was not only restrained due to his ministerial post and the Chancellery but also by the fact that the SPD did not have a corresponding partner in Greece: PASOK was founded only after the restoration of Greek democracy and his leader Andreas Papandreou distanced himself from German Social Democrats even before 1974, while Brandt was critical of Papandreou's radical political rhetoric.[26] Rother also points to the fact that Brandt kept close ties to Spain from his time there during the Spanish Civil War (1937) and the fact that he had no connections in Greece that were equivalent to his close relations with Felipe Gonzalez and Mario Soares. For all these reasons, Greece never played a role in Brandt's international politics to match that of Spain and Portugal although it gained symbolic value as the cradle of democracy in an era of Southern European dictatorships.

After the restoration of democracy in Greece, Brand became a powerful symbol of the struggle against the colonels that still shapes the image of Germany in Greece in a very positive way. This era has been recorded in the collective memory as one of German solidarity, as was visible in a recent exhibition organised by the Friedrich Ebert Foundation (FES) and the Greek Contemporary Social History Archives (ASKI) that toured many German and Greek cities between 2017 and 2020.[27]

1 Νίκος Παπαναστασίου, Αντίσταση από μικροφώνου. Ο Παύλος Μπακογιάννης απέναντι στη δικτατορία των συνταγματαρχών [Nikos Papanastasiou, Resistance via the microphone. Pavlos Bakoyannis opposition towards the Dictatorship of the Colonels] (Athens: Papadopoulos, 2020), 112–113; see also Dimitrios Apostolopoulos, *Die griechisch-deutschen Nachkriegsbeziehungen: Historische Hypothek und moralischer Kredit. Die bilateralen politischen und ökonomischen Beziehungen unter besonderer Berücksichtigung des Zeitraums [The Greek-German Postwar Relations: Historical Hypothec and Moral Credit. The Bilateral Political and Economic Relations with special Reference to the Period 1958–1967]* (Frankfurt a. M.: Peter Lang, 2004).

2 Antonio Muñoz Sánchez, "Wandel durch Annäherung in Spanien: Willy Brandt und das Franco-Regime (1964–1975) [*Change through rapprochement in Spain: Willy Brandt and the Franco Regime*]," in: *Willy Brandt: Politisches Handeln und Demokratisierung* [*Willy Brandt: Political Action and Democratization*], ed. Frank Ettrich and Dietmar Herz (Opladen, Berlin, Toronto: Budrich UniPress, 2015), 181–216.

3 According to Muñoz Sánchez, the SPD as the governing party pursued a cautious strategy towards the southern European dictatorships, in many respects similar to its *Ostpolitik*, in order to maintain a dialogue and support a possible liberalisation. Berlin's ambivalent attitude towards the dictatorships of Salazar and Franco was criticised by the Iberian socialists because they were aware that the SPD was offering economic, political, and technical aid. See Antonio Muñoz Sánchez, "Entre solidaridad y realpolitik: La socialdemocracia alemana y el socialismo portugués de la dictadura a la democracia [Between Solidarity and Realpolitik: German Social Democracy and Portuguese Socialism from Dictatorship to Democracy]," in: *Hispania Nova*, no. 15 (2017), 243–273; Antonio Muñoz Sánchez, *El SPD y el PSOE de la dictadura a la democracia* [*The SPD and the PSOE – Spanish Socialist Workers' Party – from Dictatorship to Democracy*] (Barcelona: RBA Libros), 2012; and also Antonio Muñoz Sánchez, "La Socialdemocracia alemana y el Estado Novo [*German Social Democracy and the Estado Novo*] (1961–1974)," in: *Portuguese Studies Review* 13, no. 1–2 (2005), 477–503.

4 Papanastasiou, *Antistasi* (2020), 15–16.

5 Βάιος, Καλογριάς, "Τα γερμανικά κόμματα και η ελληνική μεταπολίτευση. Οι σχέσεις της SPD και της CDU με το ΠΑΣΟΚ και τη Νέα Δημοκρατία [Vaios Kalogrias, *The German Parties and the Relations of the SPD and CDU with PASOK and New Democracy after 1974 (1974–1981)*]," in: Ελλάδα και Ψυχρός Πόλεμος. Επεκτείνοντας τις ερμηνείες [*Greece and the Cold War. Expanding the interpretations*], ed. Νίκος Μαραντζίδης [Nikos Marantzidis], Ιάκωβος Μιχαηλίδης [Iakovos Michailidis], Ευάνθης Χατζηβασιλείου [Evanthis Hatzivassiliou] (Thessaloniki: Epikentro, 2018), 234; and Papanastasiou, *Antistasi* (2020), 260–261.

6 Papanastasiou, ibid. 15, 140–141; see also Σπύρος Δραΐνας, *Ο Ανδρέας στη φυλακή και την εξορία. Χούντα, Αντίσταση, Αμερικανοί, Καραμανλής* [Spyros Drainas (Stan Draenos), *Andreas in Prison and Exile. Junta, Resistance, Americans, Karamanlis*] (Athens: Efimerida ton Syntakton, 2017), 213.

7 Kalogrias, *Kommata* (2018), 236–237.

8 Helmut Schmidt, *Menschen und Mächte* (Munich: Panthon, 2011 – 2nd ed.), 241.

9 Muñoz Sánchez, *Wandel* (2015), 181–182.

10 Papanastasiou, *Antistasi* (2020), 261.

11 Ibid., 149–150; and Auswärtiges Amt (Hansen), IA 4-80 SE, 21.6.1968, Politisches Archiv des Auswärtigen Amts, B26, Vol. 419.

12 Ibid.; see also Nikos Papanastasiou, "The Bavarian Greek Radio Programme for Greek Migrants and its Impact on Greek-German Relations, 1967–1974," in: *The Greek Junta and the International System: A Case Study of Southern European Dictatorships, 1967–*

74, ed. Antonis Klapsis et al. (London: Routledge, 2020), 58–70.
13 'Große Koalition' between the conservative Union – itself comprising the Christian Democratic Union (CDU) and the Christian Social Union in Bavaria (CSU) – with the Social Democrats as a junior partner.
14 Papanastasiou, *Antistasi* (2020), 155–163.
15 Alexander Clarkson, *Fragmented Fatherland. Immigration and Cold War Conflict in the Federal Republic of Germany, 1945–1980* (New York: Berghahn, 2013), 124.
16 Kalogrias, *Kommata* (2018), 237–238; see also Nikos Papanastasiou, "Griechische Politiker im Exil (1967–1974) und die Zusammenarbeit zwischen der CDU und der 'Nea Dimokratia' nach dem Fall der Obristen-Diktatur [Greek Politicians in Exile (1967–1974) and the Cooperation between the CDU and 'Nea Dimokratia' after the end of the Colonel's dictatorship]", in: *Aspekte neugriechischer Geschichte: Gesammelte Aufsätze*, ed. Heinz Richter (Wiesbaden: Harrasowitz, 2019).
17 Antonio Muñoz Sánchez, *Von der Franco-Diktatur zur Demokratie: Die Tätigkeit der Friedrich-Ebert-Stiftung in Spanien* (Bonn: Dietz, 2013); see also Peter Birle and Antonio Muñoz Sánchez, *Partnerschaft für die Demokratie: Die Arbeit der Friedrich-Ebert-Stiftung in Brasilien und Portugal* (Bonn: Dietz, 2020).
18 "Platz des Jammerns", *Der Spiegel*, Vol. 9/26. 2.1968, 28–29
19 Papanastasiou, *Antistasi* (2020), 151.
20 Ibid.
21 Papanastasiou, *Antistasi* (2020), 152–154.
22 Ibid.; see also Effie Pedaliu, "Human Rights and International Security: The International Community and the Greek Dictators," in: *International History Review 38*, no. 5 (2016), 3.
23 Papanastasiou, *Antistasi* (2020), 154
24 The escape to Germany, on a German Air Force plane of Law Professor, Giorgos-Alexandros Mangakis, who had been arrested and convicted for his opposition to the Greek Junta, caused a major rift in Greek-German relations. In April 1972, the reaction of the junta reached the point of declaring the German ambassador to Athens, Peter Limbourg, persona non grata; ibid., 236–243.
25 Antonio Muñoz Sánchez, *Von der Franco-Diktatur zur Demokratie: Die Tätigkeit der Friedrich-Ebert-Stiftung in Spanien [From Franco's Dictatorship to Democracy: The Activities of the Friedrich-Ebert-Stiftung in Spain]* (Bonn: Dietz, 2013).
26 Bernd Rother, "Willy Brandt und der griechische Widerstand [Willy Brandt and the Greek Resistance]," Symposium der Vereinigung der deutsch-griechischen Gesellschaften [lecture in the symposium of the Association of Greek-German Communities]: Der Widerstand gegen die Diktatur der Obristen (1967–1974) in Deutschland. Beispiel für einen solidarischen Kampf der griechischen und deutschen Demokraten) [The Resistance against the Dictatorship of the Colonels (1967–1974) in Germany. Example of a Struggle in Solidarity between Greek and German Democrats] 18–19 November 2016.
27 "Αλληλεγγύη και Αντίσταση. Η στήριξη της ελληνικής αντίστασης ενάντια στη στρατιωτική χούντα από τα γερμανικά κόμματα, συνδικάτα και πολιτικά ιδρύματα (1967–1974)" ["Solidarity and Resistance. The Support of the Greek Resistance against the Military Junta by German Parties, Trade Unions and Political Foundations (1967–1974)"].

Hans Peter Schunk

On Hair Police, Political Pornographers and Devourers of Communists: German Press about the Greek Military Dictatorship (1967–1974)

This essay is an abridged version of a chapter in the author's dissertation and aims to shed light on the extent to which press products, as part of 'public opinion'[1], acted as a catalyst, influencing and shaping German foreign policy with regards to the Greek military dictatorship. Furthermore, it will be shown which consequences the reporting had for social discourses. Central 'leading media outlets'[2] of the Federal Republic (*Der Spiegel, Stern, Zeit, SZ, FAZ* and the *Bayernkurier*) are selected and fully analysed. A special awareness of moral issues in foreign policy arose at the time in question due to the temporal distance to the Nazi era and the increasing politicisation at the beginning of the "red decade"[3], sharpened by the haunting television images of the atrocities committed in Vietnam, which were broadcast almost live into the nation's living rooms.[4] Contrarily, the German government's policy towards Greece was predominantly shaped by economic and security interests and therefore adopted a moderate negotiating tone.[5] Outside the government, however, numerous actors and individuals showed solidarity with the struggle of many Greeks against the junta. Thus, the author's dissertation proposes, among other things, the hypothesis that the German confrontation with the military dictatorship represents an important German-Greek 'space for collective memory' that should be further illuminated.

In this context, the German press, besides trade unions, radio broadcastings and students, acted as a hinge between German society and politics.

First reactions

The majority of the German press was thoroughly taken aback by the societal rupture of the European cultural nation, although Greece could hardly look back on stable phases at any time in the 20th century: the daily broadsheet *Frankfurter Allgemeine Zeitung* (*FAZ*) spoke of the military dictatorship as a "shock" and a "burden for the Western world" and concluded that the overthrow could not remain without consequences.[6] Likewise, *Süddeutsche Zeitung* (*SZ*) came to the same conclusion that the "fascist games" in Greece must have policy consequences.[7] Only the *Bayernkurier*, one of the few international media outlets to adopt the narrative spread by the junta of an imminent communist coup, took the position from the outset that Greece had previously been a "corrupted" democracy. In a sympathetic, anti-communist stance, the journal wrote: "the coup is the logical response to the failure of the democratic forces in the Kingdom of the Hellenes."[8] After a month, *Der Spiegel* criticised that even newspapers with more moderate attitudes were soft-pedalling the situation in Greece:

> "In German newspapers and under the 'patronage of the military' ('Schwarzwälder Bote'), 'calm' returned to the Greek country shortly after the coup. In Athens, 'normal everyday life' prevailed again and 'life pulsated everywhere in the city', reported 'Bremer Nachrichten' four days after the coup, according to dpa."[9]

Meanwhile, regarding foreign policy dimensions, the historian and journalist Sebastian Haffner pointed out in *Stern* that the Danes and Norwegians would be "fully within their rights if they wanted to raise the issue of the Greek coup plotters 'disregard for democracy and constitutional freedoms' in the NATO Council" since Greece was part of "our own club" and had committed itself to the rule of law through ratification. The United States, as the leading NATO power, had practical options for changing the course of events in Greece, but persisted in "conflict aversion", which Haffner illustrated with the Suez crisis of 1956, when:

> "two far stronger NATO members, England and France, acted in breach of another treaty obligation – that of Article 1. – to refrain from any threat or use of force in their international relations – America had only to make the faint suggestion of a currency boycott and the incident was resolved."[10]

Boycott or not?

Especially in the first two years of the dictatorship, there was a public discussion about whether Greece was still an appropriate holiday destination, given the circumstance. *FAZ* first printed the call for a boycott and the strong condemnations by the actress Irene Papas: "Nazism has risen again in Greece. The radical little group of half-educated colonels who want to lift Greece's morale with their machine guns has turned out to be a gang of blackmailers."[11] A few months later, however, another article explicitly advised against boycotting Greece, saying that the poor and ordinary people of Greece should not be deprived of their only source of income:

> "'Greece concerns us' – the slogan has become common coin throughout Europe in recent months. In our opinion, besides its deep political truth, it also contains an invitation to consider visiting the beautiful country."[12]

During an interview in a Cologne hotel in June 1969, the *Stern* magazine confronted the junta-friendly conservative politician Werner Marx of the governing Christian Democratic Union (CDU) with the famous oppositional Greek actress Melina Mercouri, without his prior knowledge. After Marx had painted a positive picture of Greece, predicting that Greek tourism would see a 400 per cent increase, *Stern* replied: "If now, as you have outlined, Dr. Marx, many tourists come to Greece, wont [Deputy Prime Minister] Mr. Pattakos then say, just like Adolf Hitler in 1936: 'Look here, the world is our guest!'?"[13] Especially in the first months of the Colonels' rule, tourists were forbidden to wear miniskirts, which exemplifies why there were great reservations about travelling to Greece. In addition, "hair raids" were carried out against long-haired men, as reported in *Der Spiegel*, sardonically echoing the views of the prudish junta on the "phenomenon of decadent hippiedom" which the military regime was cracking down on: "But as an expression of an international decadence movement such as hippiedom, long hair ceases to be a matter of personal taste and becomes a social issue."[14] *Bayernkurier*, on the other hand, demonstratively promoted Greece as a travel destination:

> "Athens' holiday planners rely on several factors of recovery. German Finance Minister Strauß called the Greek currency the most stable in the world [...] Corfu is the insider tip of 1968."[15]

Reports on injustice in Greece and problems in the Federal Republic of Germany

Der Spiegel devoted itself fervidly to the topic of Greece with numerous multi-page reports, and two cover stories. In August 1967, *Stern* photographer Fred Ihrt even risked his life when he flew on behalf of the magazine from Beirut to the prison island of Jaros with the help of a Lebanese pilot in a daring investigative action to prove the existence of concentration camps there. Despite the surveillance of Greek airspace, he was able to take impressive photos by flying very low, pictures which future reports and politicians often relied on.[16] Furthermore, a particularly unique feature of *Süddeutsche Zeitung* was extensive reporting on the junta's 'purges' (dismissals in the civil service, etc.) and arrests, as well as penal sentences throughout the period of the military dictatorship. Strikingly, they even managed to report about comparatively minor incidences, such as the arrest of merely two generals or a handful of opposition students. Through this performative act, the injustice perpetrated by the military dictatorship remained in the public eye. Most of the newspapers examined also conducted many interviews with high-ranking military officers and important personalities of the Greek public. On the one hand, this created an awareness of the persecuted status of opposition members, and, on the other hand, it revealed the crude *weltanschauung* held by the junta representatives. In an interview with the *Der Spiegel*, the eccentric Deputy Prime Minister Stylianos Pattakos dehumanised communists, claiming that "communists are beasts". To the objection that as an Orthodox Christian believer one should not distinguish between different groups of people, he merely replied: "We only make a distinction between human beings and beasts."[17] Despite that statement, later in the interview he denied the use of torture against communists and opposition activists: "If you show me someone who has been tortured by our police, I will shoot myself."[18] As the *Der Spiegel* conducted interviews with him, the journal itself tried to reveal his inconsistencies:

> "When Der Spiegel reminded Deputy Prime Minister and Minister of the Interior Pattakos of his promise to investigate any specific torture complaint, the tank general declared himself incompetent and referred the matter to the prosecutor at the military court."[19]

Die Zeit not only conducted numerous interviews but also provided a personal platform for critics of the regime by publishing entire articles verbatim (eg by Eleni Vlachou[20], Andreas Papandreou[21], Wassilis Filias[22]), thus making an active contribution to the resistance movement against the military dictatorship. An important concern of *Der Spiegel* and *Die Zeit* in particular was to report on the individual fates (and the underlying system) of Greeks who had suffered imprisonment and torture. In order to strikingly and vividly show readers the atrocities committed by and the overall character of the regime, *Der Spiegel's* interviews and reports covered almost two dozen types of torture and humiliation.[23] Additionally, extensive reports covered Greek guest workers in West Germany being spied on, monitored, and sometimes dismissed for giving critical statements – or often simply due to membership in a German trade union.[24] Some anecdotes reveal the underhandedness with which the Greek government took action against Greeks in Germany: "For example, one guest worker and trade union member was suddenly informed of the death of his mother. He then went home and was arrested on arrival."[25]

Numerous testimonies demonstrated the consequences of the appeal by Social Councillor[26] Flokos on 20 July 1967 in which he called on workers' committees to report and monitor "enemies of Greece". *Die Zeit* concluded: "It is fairly certain that the Athens government is expanding a network of informants on German soil directed against its own countrymen."[27] The Federal Foreign Office (Auswärtiges Amt, AA) however did not see enough valid evidence for such a statement, despite ample circumstantial evidence.[28] *Stern* also addressed the pattern refusing to extend or outright withdrawal of passports of regime critics; German authorities, too, were not always cooperative in issuing aliens' passports or granting asylum. This was exemplified by the case of the southern district town of Zirndorf, near Nuremburg. The weekly's overall conclusion was the following:

> "German treaty loyalty and bureaucratic narrow-mindedness help the Greek embassy and the six consulates-generals in their fight against opponents of the regime on German soil."[29]

Especially until 1970, various problems arose on German soil due to countless clashes between Greek regime supporters and opponents. Many activities were limited to distributing leaflets against the junta or defacing consulates, but sometimes disruptions of celebrations escalated into brawls or even open street fights. With reports from Düsseldorf, Munich, Frankfurt, Hanover, and Aschaffenburg, *Stern*, for example, tried to warn of further eruptions of tension that could result.[30] Moreover, there were isolated acts of sabotage (firebombs against a freight train)[31] and attempted bomb attacks, for example on a travel agency of a regime loyalist in Munich.[32] In addition to the Bavarian Minister of the Interior, Bruno Merk, who saw such clashes in the Munich area as "endangering the security of the population"[33], the *Münchner Tageszeitung* (TZ) in an article entitled "No place for bombers" demanded to "[e]nd the underground fighting of foreign fanatics".[34] Greek officials, however, did their bit to inflame the situation further. Relentlessly, despite perpetual pleas from the AA to stop it, the anniversary of the coup was ostentatiously celebrated.

Due to the disturbances, the Greek Consul General Papageorgiou remarked wryly to the AA, "unfortunately the current political constellation does not allow Greek tanks to be laid out against recalcitrant Greek guest workers."[35] Even more impressive is the fact that in 1969, the official chauffeur of the Consulate General to Frankfurt, Joannis Rossis, as a demonstration of power, pulled out a Walther PPK pistol in front of regime opponents at a demonstration in Döringheim in Hesse and cocked it, as reported by *Der Spiegel*.[36]

Polemic criticism

Die Zeit elaborated on the arbitrary nature of the Greek justice system by contrasting two infamous cases. On the one hand, on 20 September 1967, a girl in Thessaloniki was sentenced to four years' imprisonment because she listened to banned records by the left-wing music icon Mikis Theodorakis. On the other hand, the defendants in the 'Iraklion Trial' of 21 March 1968 (the passenger ship *Iraklion* had sunk in a storm on the voyage from Crete to Piraeus, killing 241 people), only received a six-year prison sentence, despite proof that the ship's safety had been deliberately neglected for profit-seeking motives. *Die Zeit* therefore judged the overall judicial system sharply and polemically: "In political matters, however, things are very freislerisch [after the famous Nazi judge Roland Freisler – H. P. S]."[37]

Several articles attempted to place the Greek junta in the same category as National Socialism. The image of the 'fascist' military government was created through the choice of content and the language used. In some places, however, this categorisation was achieved more or less directly with simple polemical methods. In an interview in October 1967, CDU politician Erik Blumenfeld, one of the first German MPs to travel to Greece and with a relatively uncritical stance towards the regime, made a statement about Deputy Prime Minister Pattakos' peculiar sense of humour, to which *Die Zeit* retorted: "Like Hermann Göring's humour?"[38] It is striking that *Die Zeit* used the word "fascist" in many articles referencing the regime in Athens.[39] Moreover, in some places, the "totality"[40] or the "right-wing radicalism"[41] of the junta were elaborated upon. Such formulations were also frequently found in the other newspapers examined for the present analysis.

Generally characteristic of the language used, however, is the fact that most of the newspapers critical of the junta used sharp, often polemical language. Pattakos is called a "junta buffoon"[42] in *Der Spiegel*, Greece is classified as a "banana republic,"[43] and the members of the military government are called "devourers of communists"[44]. Statements such as "terror reigns in Greece,"[45] headlines such as "Despotism of the authorities,"[46] reports on the "militant iron-eaters"[47] or the previously cited banana republic reference[48] do not make *Die Zeit*'s reporting any less trenchant. While the *FAZ* and *SZ* tried to use neutral language whenever possible, the intentionally sharp attacks in the *Stern* coverage mostly spoke for themselves. Polemical criticism in *Bayernkurier* was mainly directed at "leftists" and "intellectuals". Protest musician Mikis Theodorakis was disparagingly called a "propagandist",[49] opposition activist Andreas Papandreou was compared to Goebbels,[50] German journalist Günter Wallraff's 'self-anchoring' as a protest for human rights on Syntagma Square was captioned "Political clown in Athens".[51] However, Günter Grass was the subject of the most over-the-top coverage. In a veritable tirade, Grass was defamed for his critical stance on Greece, called a "hate speaker" and, six months later, a "political pornographer."[52] The speech Grass gave at Athens University in the spring of 1972 was described as a "rhetorical rampage" in which he offered "the alleged fascists in Athens [...] an example of West German left-wing fascist thinking."[53] Since Chancellor Brandt was informed about Grass' trip, the *Bayernkurier* opined in this case: "Chancellor Brandt should have spared the Greeks from listening to him. Suffice it to say that in 1973, at the latest, the German electorate will have to hear him again, on behalf of the SPD."[54] In case of *Bayernkurier*, criticism of left-wing public figures was always – as the last example explicitly shows – representative of criticism of the federal government in general and of Brandt individually. Brandt was accused of adopting a cool and reserved attitude towards Athens, thus damaging the traditionally good German-Greek relations.[55] Since the Social Democratic leader also depended on Greece's vote for solidarity funding for Berlin, he was accused of double standards:

> "Why, however, do Willy Brandt's party friends not protest, who railed so loudly against the Athens government

at the time and only recently again, when Greece's voice could be used so well and was so much needed, since Berlin is at stake? Domestic and foreign policy on the Peloponnese should be distinguished? This could have been foreseen earlier. Whoever speaks like this today is using double standards."[56]

The question of the (economic) relationship

Bayernku*rier* saw the long-term consequences of this badly perceived policy towards Greece explicitly in the fact that the new civilian Prime Minister Markezinis had mentioned the good relations with France and Great Britain in his first speech in autumn 1973, but did not mention the Federal Republic of Germany at all.[57] Moreover, according to the monthly magazine, Germany's European neighbours had already economically overtaken it in Greece years before, although or precisely *because* they adopted a indulgent attitude in dealing with the Greek junta.[58] In the conspicuously intensive reporting on financial and economic policy – in accordance with *FAZ*'s general profile – an indirect, critical attitude that Bonn's policy endangered economic interests occasionally surfaced:

> "It is not least the [political] climate that causes difficulties for interested German parties in their negotiations in Greece. [...] Many promising large-scale projects in which there was fundamental German interest were ultimately realised by [other] foreign companies [...] Politics has played into economic relations. [...] The sting of being shunned by Germany is deeply felt on the Greek side."[59]

Furthermore, weapons supply and guaranteed defence aid were central points of criticism of Bonn's policy towards Greece. Even though a number of the newspapers examined in this contribution addressed the issue of arms deliveries, *Stern* magazine must be highlighted at this point. In an article about the delivery of four submarines from Howaldt-Werke, which would be necessary "to secure the alliance," *Stern*, according to its own statement, deconstructed a "legend": contrary to the information given by the Federal Ministry of Economics and the AA, the individual parts manufactured in Germany were not only not in accordance with Western European Union (WEU) law, but the warships were to be delivered to Athens fully assembled, which was forbidden.[60] In the course of the uprising at the Polytechnic in November 1973, which was violently put down by the junta, *Stern* sharply criticised German arms deliveries:

> "With the approval of Chancellor Willy Brandt, 100,003 small arms, 3,000 submachine guns and ammunition were delivered from the Federal Republic to the Athens government two months before the bloody clashes between the Greek civilian population and the military junta [...]."[61]

By contrast, *Bayernkurier* pointed out that Greece, due to its dire equipment situation and foreign exchange problems, urgently needed German arms aid in order to guarantee the security of NATO's south-eastern flank. In an interview, a high-ranking military officer explained to the *Bayernkurier* readership that German Leopard battle tanks specifically could remedy the previously mentioned precarious situation.[62]

Problematic representation

The guideline of the AA was that top politicians and high-ranking officers should refrain from official trips to Greece. The aim was to prevent Greece from receiving a symbolic boost at the international level,[63] and:

> "In both the bilateral and multilateral spheres, decisions are to be taken from which public opinion can infer how the federal government is disposed towards the military regime in Greece."[64]

In the summer of 1968, the trip to Greece of four conservative and two liberal politicians and their wives at the expense of the junta attracted a lot of attention.[65] At a press conference held in Athens for this purpose, several journalists from major German newspapers criticised the acceptance of this vacation offer as well as the junta-friendly attitude of the MPs in general. Henri Nannen – the editor of *Stern* – commented on the parliamentarians' less than insightful answers, stating that this was the "the onset of corruption"; subsequently, two members of the Bundestag left the room in consternation.[66] Consequently, the AA had to deal with the matter both internally as well as in the Bundestag.[67] Josef Ertl (Free Democratic Party – FDP) was even forced to justify his position in a letter to the editor of *SZ*, while Josef Stecker (Christian Democratic Union – CDU) had previously defended himself to the SPD (Social democratic) press service and rejected criticism of his actions.[68]

Furthermore, trips by individual conservative politicians continued to attract the attention of the newspapers. For *Die Zeit*, Werner Marx's plea during a stay in Athens for a "grace period" for the junta, along with his demand for the continuation of military aid, marked a further, "scandalous variant" of the debate.[69] The trip of the junta-friendly CDU MP Erik Blumenfeld was also rebuked in the *FAZ*: "Summa summarum, the MP was the best advocate a totalitarian regime could ever find in Western Europe."[70] *Der Spiegel* even attributed a pioneering role to Blumenfeld's visit since his trip effectively increased the goodwill of West German right-wing parliamentarians for the junta.[71] In contrast, while the trips of SPD MPs did attract the attention of the press, they were not criticised to the same extent.[72] Furthermore, a trip to Greece by a Bavarian delegation of 80 people (conservative MPs, entrepreneurs and financiers) to Athens to establish economic cooperation was also reported. The official line of the Bonn government was quoted in *Der Spiegel*: "Out of consideration for public opinion, Bonn politicians rejected official invitations to visit the dictatorship state. The Bavarians, of course, thought differently."[73] When Franz Sackmann, Secretary of State in the Bavarian Ministry of Economic Affairs, had previously travelled to Greece to establish closer economic ties with the junta (in the course of which he denounced German reporting), the *Spiegel* stated, that Sackmann saw this policy a "corrective to Willy Brandt's foreign policy"[74]. The monopoly on interpreting public opinion was also fiercely contested. The editor of *Handelsblatt*, Friedrich Vogel, tried to get positive stories for his newspaper because he saw the anti-communist junta as a useful and reliable economic partner. Vogel, at the same time President of the Union of the European Business and Financial Press, flew to Athens with a delegation to promote the export of capital, where he thanked Papadopoulos with a gift. In order to continue improving economic relations, a brochure was published in Germany immediately after the trip on the second anniversary of the coup. In it, Greece's situation was clearly embellished and Vogel bluntly stated:

> "I am certainly not letting you in on a secret by pointing out that it is precisely in the borderlands between business and politics that the interested parties are located who, equipped with often considerable funds, try to influence public opinion in their favour."[75]

Public opinion in the diplomatic framework

German public opinion was clearly a thorn in the side of the junta. The travels of junta-friendly politicians and businessmen were therefore always used by the regime to order publication of negative quotes about German media in all major Greek newspapers. In addition, on numerous occasions the junta expressed its "discomfort with the attitude of large sections of the German public and the German mass media towards the internal Greek situation"[76] to German diplomats, politicians, and business representatives. On top of this, the Greek Ambassador in Bonn, Alexis Kyrou, wrote directly to Brandt, accusing the press organs of the Confederation of German Trade Unions (DGB) and the Social Democratic Party of Germany (SPD) to directly interfere in Greek domestic politics.[77] Particularly sharp criticism was sometimes expressed via the Greek press. After a critical report in *Der Spiegel* about a trial in Athens, the mouthpiece[78] of the junta, *Nea Politia*, reacted with the following demand:

> "If Der Spiegel behaves in a Nazi manner, it is the duty of German public opinion to distance itself from this dissolute magazine. We await the reaction of the official representatives of the German people, that is, the Bundestag, the Federal Government and the parties. We Greeks believe that the German people unreservedly condemn the attitude of Der Spiegel."[79]

From the German side, too, public opinion was repeatedly mentioned at the diplomatic level. After the unsuccessful coup by King Constantine and a large-scale amnesty at the end of 1967, which had been announced beforehand but was not granted, the AA feared a critical attitude from the media when working relations were resumed at the beginning of 1968. German Ambassador Schlitter therefore told the Greek Foreign Minister: "since public opinion now has an influence on inter-state relations," he had to draw attention to the non-implementation of this amnesty.[80] Chancellor Brandt was also instructed by the AA to mention during a conversation with the Greek Foreign Minister in New York in 1968 that events by Greek politicians in exile in Germany were "consistently approved by public opinion and must not be prevented due to our constitution."[81]

By autumn 1969, an increasingly negative image of Greece had developed within the media landscape. Press reports and protests increasingly articulated the demand for Greece to be excluded from the Council of Europe. The new German ambassador in Athens, Peter Limbourg, was thus asked by the AA to point out the conciliatory position of the German government to Prime Minister Papadopoulos during the presentation of his credentials. At the meeting of the Committee of Ministers of the Council of Europe in London in May 1969, the complaining states had been urged by Brandt to show moderation, so Limbourg was instructed to honour that position: "Depending on the course of the conversation, you may infer, when appropriate, that this [moderation] must not be taken for granted, given German public opinion and this year's Bundestag elections."[82] All this took place against the backdrop of demands in the press for Greece's exclusion, with appeals such as:

> "If it is agreeable to this country to treat the credibility of its system and its political representatives as a weighty criterion, Bonn's attitude towards Athens is precisely the case where morality should be asked first and usefulness second – by the government."[83]

The significant influence of the critical stance of the press can be illustrated by the Bonn government's eventual opting for Greece's suspension from the Council of Europe, before which several hundred petitions had reached the Chancellery.[84] Chancellery Minister Ehmke informed Brandt in a letter at the beginning of December 1969 that, due to public pressure, no other position could be taken than to vote for Greece's exclusion. He commented on this in a letter saying: "We would not be able to maintain any other position in terms of domestic politics and within the party."[85]

Numerous archived letters from this period addressed to Brandt and Foreign Minister Scheel refer to newspaper reports, for example the letter from an FDP member to Scheel: "In 'Der Spiegel' of 8.12., however, I read that you are still not determined to exclude the Greek dictators from the Council of Europe. This is absolutely incomprehensible to me."[86]

Impact

One immediate consequence of the reporting was the expulsion of German journalists from Greece who reported unfavourably about the junta: Eva Götz (*NZZ, Frankfurter Rundschau, Kölner Stadtanzeiger*), Baldur Bockhoff (*SZ, Weserkurier, Die Zeit*) and Kostas Tsatsaronis (*Der Spiegel*). Heinz Gstrein, correspondent of *Rheinischer Merkur* and editor of a book critical of the Greek regime, was arrested on the street, beaten, and interrogated.[87] Tsatsaronis was offered a double salary before his arrest and expulsion if he would adopt a junta-friendly course, which he refused.

The PR agency hired by the junta also organised free trips for German journalists, *Der Spiegel* revealed in a 1976 report. A total of twelve journalists accepted the offer and flew to Athens or received cash payments and dinners for junta-friendly articles, including the deputy editor-in-chief of the tabloid *Bild*, Peter Meyer-Ranke. Peter Hornung (who had called Grass a "political pornographer") of *Bayernkurier* must be singled out here as he was particularly courted by the junta and his articles clearly bear the hallmarks of his promise to report particularly positively on the military government.[88]

Moreover, such reporting indirectly influenced historical scholarship. The historian Heinz A. Richter, who has published more than 20 books on the history of Cyprus and Greece, used articles from *Der Spiegel* as a source in almost 20 percent of the footnotes in his depiction of the military dictatorship up until the uprising at the Polytechnic.[89]

German Emergency Acts

It is noteworthy that the topic of Greece also found its way into broader West German discourse. The widespread social debate about the proposed German Emergency Acts (*Notstandsgesetze*), in which basic rights could be restricted in situations of crisis, is closely linked to the period examined in this article. Just two weeks after the coup, *Der Spiegel* specifically linked the two topics of the proposed Emergency Acts and the Greek junta regime, calling attention to concerning parallels and to the dangers the Greek situation demonstrated in terms of a potential abuse of such restrictive laws.[90]

Additionally, references can be found elsewhere linking the Greek state of siege to the German Emergency Acts.[91] The APO student movement (*Außerparlamentarische Opposition* – 'extra-parliamentary opposition') protested against this restriction of basic rights and expressed concern about a potential abuse of power by the government and the possibility of another Ermächtigungsgesetz ('Enabling Act', as Hitler's consolidation of power was called). A left-wing faction of SPD, which identified dangers in the proposed law, also drew on the practices of the Greek military government as a cautionary example.[92] At the government level, Horst Ehmke explained the sudden loss of public confidence in the Emergency Acts as early as July 1967 as follows: "The events in Greece and during the Shah's visit have unfortunately rapidly worsened the mood for the emergency discussion."[93]

Even the Greek side made reference to the topic of the Emergency Acts. In an interview with *Der Spiegel* at the end of 1968, the Greek government spokesman Vyron Stamatopoulos stated that Papadopoulos still wanted to govern with a modified state of siege but that its new provisions were: "no less democratic than the German Emergency Acts".[94]

The importance of Greece for the student movement

Alongside trade unions and radio broadcasts of *Deutsche Welle* and *Bayerischer Rundfunk*, university students played a special role in the struggle and protest against the junta in Germany. In the historical specialist literature on the student movement, however, the topic of Greece received far less attention than its significance would suggest.[95] Even on Wikipedia, Greece is not mentioned in the corresponding article.[96] However, if one looks at the public discourse and press reports of the time, a completely different picture emerges. Protesting the Greek junta was mentioned in numerous articles as equally important to the student movement as Vietnam, the Emergency Acts, and the so-called encrusted structures of German society. Greece was thus a key topic indicative of the nature of the student protests, as the following selections aptly illustrate:

> "[The protesting] students in West Germany [...] are against the war in Vietnam, the Greek military dictatorship, against the Emergency Acts and nuclear armament, against the police truncheon."[97]

> "Germany's students have no subject except the thorny university reform, only abstracts far away in Greece, Persia, Vietnam, China – mostly countries they know only from print."[98]

Furthermore, dozens[99] of other passages in newspaper articles report on students who articulated their protest against the junta or the course of the federal government, or supported Greek guest workers. Protest against the military dictatorship also ranked high in letters to the editor, such as that of a reader from Munich to *SZ* trying to understand the essence of public accusations against students' accusations, point by point.[100]

A link to the students' everyday life further illustrates the scale of the topic: "the Association of German Student Bodies (VDS) speculated in its 'Information from the Student Body' that the Greek military dictatorship had been 'godparent' to the formulation of the CSU draft [on the university plans, H. P. S.]."[101] The general perception of the VDS was also connected to the Greece issue. In a SPD parliamentary group meeting in April 1968, MP Paul Kübler spoke about how to deal with the "indoctrinated" extra-parliamentary opposition. Helmut Schmidt then asked whether he would talk to someone who had committed a crime, to which Kübler replied he would no longer talk to the newly elected VDS executive committee because it had changed the association's character. A footnote in the protocol explained what was meant in: terms of content. The VDS had: "decided on actions against the American mission in Vietnam (call for desertion), demanded the recognition of the GDR, the breaking off of relations with the military regime in Greece, the resignation of the Federal President, and had rejected the Emergency Laws." Here, too, it becomes clear that the protest over the topic of Greece was one of the defining topics of the student revolt. As evidence of the students' statements, the footnote cited a *Spiegel* article, which underlines the catalysing effect of the media discussed above.[102]

Figurehead of the student movement Rudi Dutschke characterised the importance of Greece in a *Der Spiegel* interview as follows: "Through Greece, Vietnam also came to Europe."[103] Due to its European setting, Greece was a byword for perpetrated injustice. Simultaneously a conciliatory approach to the supposedly fascist regime appeared anachronistic in and of itself.

Conclusion

The scope of the debate on the Greek military dictatorship was significant. *Stern* magazine wanted to raise awareness of the problems of the guest workers, *Die Zeit* resisted indirectly by printing the positions of opposition activists, *Der Spiegel* directly demanded that the German government exclude Greece from the Council of Europe, and *Bayern-*

kurier promoted specific travel destinations in Greece. This excerpt shows that reporting on the military dictatorship did not remain on a purely descriptive level, but was directed at specific audiences and intended to achieve specific effects.

The effects the reports – oftentimes acting as catalysts for political action – were namely: Greece's suspension from the Council of Europe, the refraining from official trips out of consideration for public opinion, on the Greek side an expulsion of journalists and an increase of diplomatic tensions, as well as influencing social discourses in both countries. Thus, the case study of the Greek military dictatorship illustrates the function of the media as the Fourth Estate in the Federal Republic of Germany.

Regarding the student movement, this essay suggests that historical memory construction can be incomplete – in comparison with the actual contemporary image. Protests against the military dictatorship were a constituting element of the student movement in West Germany. Why the military dictatorship in general has almost disappeared from memory as a reference to protest against injustice at that time can only be speculated. One possible explanation is the prevailing memory of Vietnam and its continued pop-cultural dominance over time (Fortunate Son, Full Metal Jacket, Vietnam flashback memes, etc.), which seems to have a reciprocal effect on historiography. This essay therefore advocates for expanding the memory of protest in West Germany against injustice and atrocities by re-devoting attention to the case of Greece.

---

1 According to the German Federal Agency for Civic Education, there is no clear definition of 'public opinion'. Thus, the paper employs a pragmatic definition in which the press, as an immanent subset of 'public opinion', takes a central role in influencing the whole. Ulrich Sarcinelli, "Öffentliche Meinung," in: *Handwörterbuch des politischen Systems der Bundesrepublik Deutschland*. 7th, upd. ed., ed. Uwe Andersen, Wichard Woyke (Heidelberg: Springer VS, 2013).

2 Despite a certain difference in time: In a survey among journalists conducted in 1993, it was exactly those five selected print media (with the exception of the *Bayernkurier*)

which, with multiple responses, represented the most important 'leading media outlets' in Germany: *Spiegel* 66,7 %; *Süddeutsche Zeitung (SZ)* 46,6 %; *Stern* 37,1 %; *Frankfurter Allgemeine Zeitung (FAZ)* 36,2 %; *Die Zeit* 34,4 %. Jürgen Wilke, "Leitmedien und Zielgruppenorgane," in: *Mediengeschichte der Bundesrepublik Deutschland*, ed. Jürgen Wilke (Köln, Weimar, Wien: Böhlau, 1999), 302–329.

3 A description coined by the West German historian and former communist politician Gerd Koenen in *Das rote Jahrzehnt: unsere kleine deutsche Kulturrevolution* [*The red decade: our small German cultural revolution*], 1967–1977 (Cologne: Kiepenheuer und Witsch, 2001).

4 Timm Kroner, "*The whole world is watching: Die Bildmacht des Vietnamkriegs*" (https://nbn-resolving.org/urn:nbn:de:hebis:30:3-335873, 2014); Piers Robinson, "Theorizing the Influence of Media on World Politics: Models of Media Influence on Foreign Policy" in: *European Journal of communication 16*, no. 4 (2001), 523–544.

5 The Federal Republic of Germany (FRG) was in first place in terms of both import and export volume in Greece. Politisches Archiv des Auswärtigen Amtes [PA AA], Bestand 26, Bd. 426: StS Duckwitz an Kanzleramtschef Ehmke "Mögliche Folgen einer Suspendierung Griechenlands vom Europarat," 8 December 1969.

6 *Frankfurter Allgemeine Zeitung*, Nicolas Benkiser, "Die Diktatur in Griechenland," 8 May 1967.

7 *Süddeutsche Zeitung*, "Das Dilemma um Griechenland," 29 April 1967.

8 *Bayernkurier*, G. R., "Die Paras von Athen," 29 April 1967.

9 *Der Spiegel*, "Notstandsaktion," 8 December 1969.

10 *Stern*, Sebastian Haffner: "Gegen Demokraten helfen nur Soldaten," 21 May 1967.

11 *Frankfurter Allgemeine Zeitung*, "Für Boykott Griechenlands," 25 May 1967.

12 *Frankfurter Allgemeine Zeitung*, Karl Kerber, "Griechenland, das Regime und die Gastfreundschaft: Offener Brief aus Athen," 11 April 1968.

13 *Stern*, Werner Höfer, "Sollen Deutsche wieder nach Griechenland reisen? Die umstrittene Frage diskutieren mit Werner Höfer eine prominente griechische Emigrantin und ein deutscher Abgeordneter," 22 June 1969.

14 *Der Spiegel*, "Die haarige Flagge des Nihilismus," 15 March 1969.

15 *Bayernkurier*, Peter Hornung, "Hellas: Paradies der Inseln – Neue Epoche der Griechenland-Touristik," 13 April 1968.

16 Heinz Richter, *Griechenland 1950–1974: Zwischen Demokratie und Diktatur* (Wiesbaden: Harrassowitz, 2013), 321.

17 *Der Spiegel*, "Nur Bestien," 19 June 1967.

18 *Der Spiegel*, "Personalien," 6 May 1968.

19 *Der Spiegel*, "Vier Nägel," 24 February 1969.

20 *Die Zeit*, Eleni Vlachou, "Die Herrschaft der Obristen; Wie Griechenlands Putschisten die Freiheit verraten," 19 January 1968.

21 *Die Zeit*, Andreas Papandreou, "Das Prag der NATO," 16 May 1969.

22 *Die Zeit*, Wassilis Filias, "Widerstand im Namen Europas," 25 April 1969.

23 One report cited beatings to the point of unconsciousness, faking neck shots with blanks while put up against the wall, being locked up with "violent strumpets," or having one's hair shaved off: *Der Spiegel*, "Kahle Köpfe," 27 November 1967. Another report described electric shocks, beatings with iron bars, lighting with strong, irregular spotlights, and little or no water for days. *Der Spiegel*, "Vom Boden getrunken," 22 July 1968.

24 *Der Spiegel*, "Tür zu," 23 September 1968.

25 *Die Zeit*, Gerhard Bartels, "Das Beil des Gesetzes; Griechische Kommissionen agieren auf deutschen Arbeitsämtern," 8 September 1967.

26 The 1960 Labour Recruitment Agreement (Anwerbeabkommen) between Germany and Greece established Greek Labour Commissions (Arbeitskommissionen) in ma-

jor German cities to help Greek workers settle in. These commissions were subordinate to the Greek embassy in Bonn and received premises and support from the local German employment agencies. *Die Zeit*, Hanjo Kesting, "Zweifelhafte Arbeitskommissionen; Schwarze Listen für Athen: In Hamburg werden griechische Gastarbeiter überwacht," 7 November 1969.
27 Ibid.
28 PA AA, Bestand B 26, Bd. 413: Baron von den Brüggen an den Bundesminister der Verteidigung "Griechischer Militärattaché in Bonn," 1 September 1967.
29 *Stern*, "Kein Asyl für Griechen: Wie deutsche Behörden das Athener Militärregime unterstützen," 4 October 1970.
30 Ibid.
31 *Der Spiegel*, "Wann und wie," 10 February 1969.
32 PA AA, Bestand B 26, Bd. 413: Note des Königlich Griechischen Generalkonsulats an die Bayerische Staatsregierung, 2 October 1968.
33 PA AA, Bestand B 26, Bd. 420: Bayerischer Staatsminister des Inneren Merk an Bundesinnenminister Benda "Politische Betätigung von Exilgriechen in der Bundesrepublik Deutschland," 12 November 1968.
34 Ibid.
35 PA AA, Bestand B 26, Bd. 420: Hansen an das Referat V3 "Politische und terroristische Bestätigung von Ausländern und Emigrantenorganisationen in der Bundesrepublik Deutschland," 10 September 1968.
36 *Der Spiegel*, "Schwarze Krallen," 14 April 1969.
37 *Die Zeit*, "Justiz unter dem Militärstiefel; Athener Zwischenbilanz nach zwei Jahren," 21 February 1969.
38 *Die Zeit*, "Doch noch Hoffnung für Griechenland?" 20 October 1967.
39 An example: "In Greece, on the other hand, the wheel is being turned back. There, fascism is not moulting into freer forms of rule – it is being restored." *Die Zeit*, Theo Sommer, "Absage an die Generale; Wohin steuert Griechenland (Schluß) – Hellas gehört zu Europa, aber ohne seine Diktatoren," 6 October 1967.
40 *Die Zeit*, "ZeitSpiegel; Worte der Woche," 16 May 1969; *Die Zeit*, Karl-Heinz Janßen, "Chirurg der griechischen Demokratie"; "Gerogios Papadopoulos: Diktator ohne Geduld," 4 October 1967.
41 *Die Zeit*, "Ein Vietnam in Hellas? Das Dilemma des Königs Konstantin," 22 December 1967.
42 *Der Spiegel*, "Brief an den Boss," 3 November 1969.
43 *Der Spiegel*, "Auch mit Bart," 19 June 1967.
44 *Der Spiegel*, "Mutterliebe verboten," 25 September 1969.
45 *Die Zeit*, "Die Austreibung des Geistes," 14 July 1967; *Die Zeit*, Theo Sommer, "Hellenen-Kreuz," 4 October 1968.
46 *Die Zeit*, "Obristen-Willkür," 23 April 1973.
47 *Die Zeit*, Theo Sommer, "Ein Lichtblick," 29 November 1968.
48 *Die Zeit*, Ansgar Skriver, "Europas Bananenrepublik: Zwei Jahre Diktatur in Griechenland," 18 September 1969.
49 *Bayernkurier*, Peter Hornung, "Mikis Theodorakis will in die Heimat; Resignation eines Propagandisten," 21 October 1972.
50 *Bayernkurier*, Marcel Hepp, "Hellenische Zustände: Athen mit eigenen Augen," 25 November 1967.
51 *Bayernkurier*, Peter Hornung, "Polit-Clown in Athen," 18 May 1974.
52 *Bayernkurier*, Peter Hornung, "Mikis Theodorakis will in die Heimat; Resignation eines Propagandisten," 21 October 1972.
53 *Bayernkurier*, Peter Hornung, "Der Skandal von Athen," 1 April 1972.
54 Ibid.
55 *Bayernkurier*, Peter Hornung, "NATO-Pfeiler im Südosten," 3 October 1970.
56 *Bayernkurier*, "Schützenhilfe," 20 June 1968.
57 *Bayernkurier*, Peter Hornung, "Nun beginnt der politische Alltag; Kabinett Markezinis kündigt baldige Wahlen an," 20 October 1973.
58 *Bayernkurier*, Marcel Hepp, "Sozialis-

tische Geschäfte mit der Athener Junta; Beim Geldverdienen keine Hemmungen," 31 May 1969.
59 *Frankfurter Allgemeine Zeitung*, "Deutsche Position in Griechenland schwierig," 27 December 1972.
60 *Stern*, Peter Stähle, "Obristen unter Wasser; Die griechischen Diktatoren bekommen von Bonn komplette U-Boote geliefert," 12 April 1970.
61 *Stern*, "Bonner Hilfe für Athen," 29 November 1973.
62 *Bayernkurier*, Peter Hornung, "Eine Armee ohne Illusionen; An der Südost-Flanke der NATO," 16 November 1968.
63 PA AA, Bestand B26, Bd. 415: Aufzeichnung Schwörbel, "Die deutsche Haltung gegenüber Griechenland," 24 August 1967.
64 Akten zur Auswärtigen Politik der Bundesrepublik Deutschland [AA PD], 1967, Dok. 308, "Aufzeichnungen des Ministerialdirigenten Böker" (24 August 1967), 1223.
65 The British media agency *Maurice Fraser* organised the trip, commissioned by the Greek government to enhance the regime's international reputation. See *Der Spiegel*, "Eine Troika von Mulis," 30 September 1968.
66 PA AA, Bestand 26, Bd. 413: Fernschrieben Ahrens ans Auswärtige Amt "Besuch deutscher Abgeordneter in Griechenland," 1 August 1968.
67 PA AA, Bestand 26, Bd. 413: Kanzleramtsreferent Boss an Ministerbüroleiter Ritzel "Griechenland; hier: Besuch von Abgeordneten der CDU und FDP (Drahtbericht der Botschaft Athen Nr. 248 vom 2. August 1968)," 5 August 1968.
68 *Süddeutsche Zeitung*, Josef Ertl, "Als deutscher Parlamentarier in Athen," 10/11 August 1968.
69 *Die Zeit*, Rolf Binner, "Das Jahr der Obristen; Eine griechische Bilanz" 19 April 1968.
70 *Frankfurter Allgemeine Zeitung*, Georg Achaios, "Politische Häftlinge in Griechenland," 4 March 1968.
71 *Der Spiegel*, "Public Relations; Dummes Salz," 12 August 1968.
72 *Der Spiegel*, "Platz des Jammerns," 26 March 1968. Der Spiegel, "Lieber baden gehen," 7 June 1971.
73 *Der Spiegel*, "Regime-Werbung; Reise gratis," 8 June 1970.
74 *Der Spiegel*, "Bessere Demokraten," 13 October 1969.
75 *Der Spiegel*, Otto Köhler, "Griechische Handelsfreiheit," 5 May 1969.
76 PA AA, Bestand B26, Bd. 413: Fernschreiben Botschafter Schlitter ans AA, 12 June 1968.
77 PA AA, Bestand B26, Bd. 415: Botschafter Kyrou an Brandt, 22 June 1967.
78 PA AA, Bestand B26, Bd. 420: Fischer ans Referat I A 4, "Unterrichtung des neuen deutschen Botschafters in Athen; hier: Griechischsprachiges Programm der Deutschen Welle," 18 September 1969.
79 *Der Spiegel*, "Zitate," 4 August 1969.
80 PA AA, Bestand B 150, Bd. 116: Fernschreiben Schlitter ans AA, 10 January 1968.
81 PA AA, Bestand B26, Bd. 412: Aufzeichnung Frank, "Besuch Herrn Minister in New York; hier: Eventuelles Gespräch mit griechischen Außenminister Pipinelis," 3 October 1968.
82 PA AA, Bestand B26, Bd. 420: Frank an Limbourg, "Gesprächsführung bei den Antrittsbesuchen in Athen," 22 September 1969.
83 *Der Spiegel*, "Wie neu ist die Bonner Republik," 8 December 1969.
84 Especially the folder PA AA, Bestand B26, Bd. 427.
85 BArch, Bestand B136 (Bundeskanzleramt), Bd. 6433: "Vermerk von Ehmke an den Bundeskanzler," 2 December 1969.
86 PA AA, Bestand B26, Bd. 427: Helmut Kramer an Scheel, 10 December 1969.
87 *Die Zeit*, Ansgar Skriver, "Europas Bananenrepublik: Zwei Jahre Diktatur in Griechenland," 18 September 1969.
88 *Der Spiegel*, "Aufwand für Veröffentlichungen," 1 November 1976.
89 Cf. Richter, *Griechenland*, 310–406.
90 In a bitingly sarcastic tone, the article comments: "This year shall finally bring us a beautiful, fully developed Emergency Law.

And behold, we cannot complain that we are not enlightened as to how easily such a state of emergency comes into being and how lively it is under its wing. Militaries arrest politicians, lock up thousands in internment camps, impose the law of exception, set up special courts. What is this – when it happens in Athens today?" See *Der Spiegel*, Otto Köhler, "Notstandsaktion," 8 May 1967.

91 *Der Spiegel*, "Notstand: Bachab schicken," 6 November 1967; *Süddeutsche Zeitung*, "Lübkes Rücktritt gefordert," 16 April 1968; Vergleich des russischen Botschafters Podgornyj der BRD mit Griechenland im Kontext der Notstandsdebatte, AAPD, 1968, Dok. 173, 653.

92 *Der Spiegel*, "Notstand durch Gesetz?" 6 November 1967.

93 *Der Spiegel*, "Schuld des Schah," 3 July 1967.

94 *Der Spiegel*, "Der Führer," 23 December 1968.

95 E. g. Koenen, *Das rote Jahrzehnt;* Norbert Frei, *1968: Jugendrevolte und globaler Protest* (extended edition, Munich: dtv, 2017).

96 Wikipedia. "Westdeutsche Studentenbewegung der 1960er Jahre." Last modified 2 January 2022. https://de.wikipedia.org/wiki/Westdeutsche_Studentenbewegung_der_1960er_Jahre (last access 19 October 2022).

97 *Der Spiegel*, "Herrn Rudi Dutschkes Umwälzung der Wissenschaft," 11 December 1967.

98 *Der Spiegel*, Rudolf Augstein, "Warum sie demonstrieren," 19 June 1967.

99 Evidence in the author's forthcoming dissertation, *Politische Beziehungen der Bundesrepublik Deutschland zu Griechenland, Portugal und Spanien 1967–1974*.

100 *Süddeutsche Zeitung*, Bernhard Karrer, "Was wirft man den Studenten vor?," 4/5 May 1968.

101 *Der Spiegel*, "Athener Format," 3 March 1969.

102 Fraktionssitzung, SPD, 29 April 1968, in: Editionsprogramm "Fraktionen im Deutschen Bundestag," SPD, 5. Wahlperiode, https://fraktionsprotokolle.de (last access 19 October 2022).

103 *Der Spiegel*, "Heiterkeit in die Revolution bringen," 3 March 1968.

Frank Bösch

Greek-German Protest: Public Commitment against Greece's Dictatorship in the Federal Republic

The collapse of Greece's democracy in 1967 was a shock to many Germans. This was primarily owing to the close political, economic and cultural relations between the two countries. After all, Greece was a NATO member that received substantial arms supplies, a member of the Council of Europe, associated with the European Economic Community, and the Federal Republic was Greece's largest trade partner.[1] Due to the classical educational canon and its status as a popular travel destination, many Germans felt closer to Greece than to those Latin American or African states where autocracies also flourished at the time. Greece, deemed the cradle of democracy, was the very place where it now broke down. In the eyes of the West German Left, Greece developed into a dystopian nightmare. Against the backdrop of the imminent emergency laws and the success of the NPD, it seemed to be a cautionary example of looming fascism in Federal Germany.

This chapter explores the emergence of various protests against the dictatorship in Greece. In particular, it argues that close Greek-German relations and the political activities of Greek migrants significantly contributed to making this dictatorship the focus of the protests early on, thus challenging both the pragmatic political course of the West German government and the Greek dictatorship itself. At the same time, this approach examines the role of the emerging espousal of human rights. Several studies emphasise that this came into being in the West during the 1970s, with the fight against Pinochet's dictatorship in Chile, the CSCE process and the establishment of Amnesty International considered important milestones.[2] Taking the Greek dictatorship as an example, I will show that a new form of advocacy for politically persecuted people took root in the Federal Republic as early as the second half of the 1960s.

In contrast to the few existing studies on Greek-German contemporary history, which examine in particular the government's foreign political approach[3], this chapter instead charts public and civil society engagement as drivers of protest. Four case studies focusing on different groups of actors and forms of communication will demonstrate how the political commitment for the victims of a foreign anti-communist dictatorship developed: civil society street protests, investigative journalist researching in Greece, the activities of Amnesty International and Greek-German broadcasting programmes. For this purpose, government documents, especially those of the Foreign Office, internal papers of NGOs including Amnesty International, the correspondence of the *Deutsche Welle* – a German tax-financed international broadcaster – as well as sources of protest movements will be analysed.

Public protests of Greek and German nationals

The fact that Greek migrants in the Federal Republic played a key role in initiating the protests can be explained in the first instance by referring to their migration background. Approximately a tenth of all Greeks left their home country, at least temporarily, over the course of the 1960s, with most of them moving to the Federal Republic. Eight per cent of the Greek population, in total more than 600,000 people, at times lived in West Germany during the wake of the 1960 recruitment agreement. During the dictatorship, this number rapidly increased because many people fled the regime.[4] For many Greeks the Federal Republic turned into a laboratory where they could speak freely about the dictatorship, organise themselves against it and transfer their experiences of democratic protest into their home country, particularly because about half of the Greek economic migrants returned to Greece. The Greek diaspora in the Federal Republic became the nucleus of broad public resistance while leading politicians of the deposed political parties rather fled to Rome, Paris and Stockholm.[5]

The Greeks' protest in West Germany had many voices as they were a socially and politically heterogenous group. Most of them were ordinary agricultural workers from the North. At the same time, students and an educated elite that taught at West German universities and made connections to academic protests came to the Federal Republic. The majority of politically active Greeks leaned towards the moderate left and was affiliated with the United Democratic Left (UDL), the party leading the protests, which had, during this time, been banned.[6] Both the outlawed Greek Communist Party and the Centrists also organised themselves in exile. Frequent conflicts arose between the political groups over the question of whether violent resistance against the dictatorship was legitimate, for instance when the radical Left planned bomb attacks on Greek Consulates in Hanover and Munich and called to fight the regime in Athens.[7] In addition, violent clashes broke out when supporters of the regime initiated counter-demonstrations, for example at an appearance of the opposition leader Andreas Papandreou in 1969.[8]

From the very beginning, Greeks and Germans protested together. Immediately after the putsch, German and Greek students gathered in front of the Greek military mission in Berlin, there were actions in the canteen of the Bonn university, in Stuttgart Greek workers and students took to the streets and in Tübingen people, including intellectuals such as Walter Jens, expressed their solidarity at Greek-German demonstrations.[9] Numerous campaigns demanding "freedom for Greece" followed, with various political groups participating, ranging from the Socialist German Student League (Sozialistischer Deutscher Studentenbund, SDS) to the Association of Christian Democratic

Students (Ring Christlich-Demokratischer Studenten, RCDS).[10] Greek and German students demonstrated by carrying posters that demanded the release of certain persons or condemned fascism in general.[11] Reports from Greece got through about the military regime oppressing alternative lifestyles, forcing men with long hair to cut it and preventing a "1968 revolution" through arrests and expelling students from university.[12] Precisely this incited the 68's protests throughout the Federal Republic even more. Discussion meetings with Greek students took place on the topic "The Example of Greece – Bourgeois Democracy and Dictatorship", emphasising the role of the Federal Republic.[13] Later protests followed in response to trials against prominent dissidents such as the musician Mikis Theodorakis.[14] Students also protested against the presence of "official Greece" in the Federal Republic, for example by blocking Greece's stall at the Frankfurt book fair. They chanted: "Fascism needs police protection" and raised banners referring to persecuted authors which read: "Here is a book RITSOS – the author is in a concentration camp." Another poster pointed to the ultraconservative censorship: "Banned in Greece: Sartre, Ionesco, Joyce, Beckett."[15] Violent protests, which included smashed windows, were also directed at the Greek embassy and consulates.[16] Particularly during 1968 in Paris, Greek and French students cooperated in a similar way.[17]

The protests against the Greek Regime of the Colonels resembled and went hand in hand with the activities against the Iranian Shah. For example, in 1968 Greek students in Hamburg went on an open-ended hunger strike to call attention to politically persecuted persons in their home country.[18] The fight against the emergency laws created a common framework for the protests. In many publications the German Left painted a picture of Greece as a model of what could soon happen in the Federal Republic. The 1968 protests were directed abroad, but predominantly accused the Western states. "Kiesinger und Brandt, auch nach Griechenland" ("Kiesinger and Brandt, move to Greece"), the protesters chanted. The fact that the coup d'état followed a plan drafted by NATO, which would also apply to the Federal Republic in case of civil unrest, added fuel to the fire of protests even in the eyes of individual CDU Bundestag members.[19]

Like the 1968 opposition as a whole, Greek dissidents in West Germany operated within international networks. From 1967 onwards, oppositional Greek students met on international congresses to discuss their opposition, and the expelled former Minister Andreas Papandreou founded the Panhellenic Liberation Movement (PAK) from his Swedish exile, which he promoted globally.[20] Andreas Papandreou, son of the minister president who was deposed in 1965, evolved internationally into the leading figure of the resistance and also gave speeches at mass meetings in the Federal Republic. Even in Western democracies, the Greeks' protest was not without danger. Reports circulated that the Greek secret service was keeping the opposition under surveillance and the Greek consulates in the Federal Republic were establishing "centres for the surveillance of its political activities", as a former staff member reported as early as 1969.[21] The new Greek government revoked the citizenship of at least 500 opposition members living in West Germany.[22]

In contrast to other student protests, several West German professors joined in criticising the Greek dictatorship. This was partly due to the close cultural and academic relationships between Germany and Greece and because some persecuted Greeks had previously worked at universities in Federal Germany. Even rather conservative professors of the law departments of Bonn, Heidelberg, Berlin and Mainz universities as well as the Rectors' Conference vigorously campaigned for the release of persecuted legal scholars such as Dimitris Tsatsos, Dimitrios Evrigenis and Georgios Mangakis and successfully offered them professorships in order for them to leave the country.[23] The arrest of four Tübingen students in Greece, among them the daughter of the cultural scientist Hermann Bausinger, resulted in broad protests of professors and intellectuals, including Ernst Bloch, Walter Jens, Martin Walser and Arno Klönne.[24] While German university professors predominantly reacted upon the persecution of colleagues, fellow academics and their families, their protest was as such directed against the dictatorship.

Prominent West German authors such as Günter Grass or Heinrich Böll also got actively involved in the protest against the Greek dictatorship. They expressed their criticism in panel debates and interviews, but also in talks at the Goethe Institute in Athens. For example, the guiding spirit of the Group 47, Hans-Werner Richter, appeared on a TV programme in 1969, together with the Greek opposition leader Andreas Papandreou, Günter Grass, Kurt Sontheimer and Arnulf Baring.[25]

West German trade unions in particular took a strong stance against the Greek autocracy. This was certainly partly due to the fact that, in contrast to Iranian or Korean migrants, many Greeks were union members.[26] The arrest of numerous trade unionists in Greece strengthened solidarity in Germany. On 28 May 1967, when general elections should have been held in Greece, the German Trade Union Confederation (Deutscher Gewerkschaftsbund, DGB) and Greek democrats organised a major protest march in Düsseldorf in favour of the restoration of human rights in Greece. During the next year, the DGB provided up to 100,000 DM for demonstrations[27] and hosted events in different places "against the Greek military dictatorship" with the exile politician Andreas Papandreou as speaker on the first anniversary of the putsch in 1968.[28] In July 1967, the government of the Federal Republic seized the suggestion of the DGB to grant asylum to Greeks whose citizenship had been revoked.[29] The IG Metall, the West German metalworkers' union, developed into a driving force of the West German-Greek protests. In solidarity with the Greek opposition, it printed its newspaper *Metall* in Greek language, and its *Ausländerreferent*, the representative for foreign workers, Max Diamant, who himself had been persecuted by National Socialism, took Greeks including Elias Hadjiandreou on board in order to bolster the fight against the Colonels. In the same vein as Amnesty International, the IG Metall compiled extensive lists of the names of prisoners, for example those of 442 "inmates of concentration camps".[30] In doing so, the trade union adopted methods used by Amnesty International.

The SPD supported these protests. Both its leadership and rank and file, which at the time enjoyed an influx of new members, became increasingly self-confident and criticised the government policy of their party comrades. Initially the parliamentary party was by no means unanimously in favour of sanctions, for example freezing the EC association.[31] The activities of the European Left strengthened the left wing of the SPD that demanded sanctions. As early as 29 June 1967, the SPD parliamentary party in the Bundestag demanded "to stop military aid for Greece until the restoration of democratic and constitutional conditions".[32] Even more substantial were calls expressed at the SPD party conference in March 1968 under the slogan "no future for dictatorships in NATO", demanding that "no weapons are delivered to Greece and that NATO military aid for Greece is suspended." In the same vein, a motion demanded that the government of the Federal Republic influenced the bodies of the European Community "to predicate any form of economic support on Greece becoming a constitutional democracy."[33] From 1967 onwards, individual SPD parliamentarians asked critical questions in the Bundestag on how the government dealt with Greece, insinuating harsher sanctions.[34] Moreover, prominent Social Democrats such as the Minister President of North Rhine-Westphalia, Heinz Kühn, and two of his state ministers supported the action group "Democracy in Greece", founded in Düsseldorf.[35] As a Social Democratic Party in the narrow sense did not exist in Greece, it remained rather unclear who the partners of the SPD were. Nevertheless, Greek dissidents and their families received substantial support payments from SPD coffers – presumably 500,000 DM in 1968. Many Social Democrats such as Willy Brandt felt reminded of persecution, expulsion and activities in exile during National Socialism. That is why Brandt himself ordered to grant residence permits to well-known oppositionists such as Andreas Papandreou or Melina Mercouri.[36]

To summarise, Greek migrants were the main drivers of the protests in the Federal Republic, but they were met with broad support from academics, intellectuals and Social Democrats.

Investigative media research

Investigative media reports from Greece written by left-liberal journalists fuelled public protests. A West German TV team that accidentally worked in Greece at the time of the putsch was able to take pictures of the night of the coup d'état.[37] Basil Mathiopoulos, a Greek journalist involved in the report who had to flee to the Federal Republic with the help of the German Foreign Office, remained an important critical voice in the German media and wrote the first book on the military putsch.[38] Journalists particularly reported about "concentration camps" on the Greek prison islands, where those in power – by their own account – had deported 6,138 political opponents in the first weeks alone. Minister of the Interior Pattakos downplayed this in public: "They are just banned on an island where they live better days than we do."[39] Even conservative West German newspapers such as the *Frankfurter Allgemeine Zeitung* (*FAZ*) were disconcerted by such statements, and left-wing journalists in their critical reports drew on analogies of National Socialism to discredit the Regime of Colonels. As early as July 1967, the news magazine *Der Spiegel* printed illustrated reports on arrests and described the "concentration camp island" Gyaros.[40] In the same year, Fred Ihrt, reporter of the current affairs magazine *Stern*, took secret aerial photographs of the prison islands in a risky operation, using a plane rented in Lebanon.[41] His pictures of barracks in the sandy wasteland were reminiscent of German National Socialist camps. *Stern* contrasted the "concentration camp report" with tourist pictures from Greece and called for a travel boycott. However, such reports could not stop international tourism to Greece, which increased in the wake of a general travel boom with charter flights and new hotel complexes, just as in Franco's Spain.[42] But this media coverage contradicted reports of the International Red Cross that only found fault with the hygiene conditions on the prison islands – a welcome vindication for the Greek Colonels. And yet, it was the known but less exposed police prisons in major cities rather than the islands that served as places of torture.[43]

Critics increasingly used National Socialism as a semantic point of reference. Greek oppositionists also referred to the "concentration camp Lakki und Lakki-Leros". Prisoners wrote to Willy Brandt "from the camp of death where the fascist military justice in Athens has incarcerated us to destroy us", urging him to stand up for the "abolishment of the extermination camps and the liberation of the tormented country".[44] It was precisely the experiences of German and Italian occupation after 1941 that propelled the Greek opposition to compare the current situation with fascism and National Socialism. In this, they followed the semantics of the 1968 movement.[45] While after visiting the prison island CDU politicians such as Erik Blumenfeld rejected comparisons with concentrations camps or Gulags, the Social Democrat Adolf Arndt argued that Leros was "a concentration camp without SS: people are destroyed little by little."[46] Comparisons with National Socialism also had repercussions on the question of the Greek government's sovereignty towards external interventions. References to "concentration camps" and thus to the "Third Reich" served to stress the necessity and legitimacy of an intervention in Greek sovereignty in order to enforce universal human rights.

West Germans who had been arrested in Greece because they had supported the opposition also reported on the use of torture in subsequent years. A young trainee lawyer from Stuttgart, who had been in custody without sentence for 15 months because of contacts to a communist,[47] described in 1973 in front of a Greek court and German journalists who had travelled to Greece that seven armed men had physically abused her already during the nightly arrest: "they beat my head and body, they clinched me."[48] In the same vein, four Tübingen students who were arrested in the same year because they had tried to smuggle a dissident out of Greece reported after their release that Greek security staff had tormented their fellow prisoners with beatings and dark standing-only cells.[49] The totalitarian violence of the Greek state was clearly not just a phenomenon of the initial years. The drastic reports substantially discredited the regime.

It was the journalist Günter Wallraff who undertook what was probably the most spectacular research to prove the use of torture in Greece. In the context of his coverage on migrant workers in German businesses he met Greeks who lived in fear of the military dictatorship. In 1971 he and some left-wing intellectuals founded the "Initiativ-Ausschuss Griechenland-Solidarität" (Initiative Committee Greece Solidarity) that advocated the release of political prisoners and democratic rights. This was followed by an action on 10 May 1974: Wallraff chained himself to a lamp post on Syntagma Square in Athens and handed out flyers critical of the regime in order to provoke an arrest. Indeed, four security guards beat his head, kidneys and genitals and marched him off.[50] Physical violence continued at the police station because he did not reveal himself to be a German journalist. When the police learned about his identity from media reports and the embassy of the Federal Republic, they stopped the violence but incarcerated him in a dirty cell until the end of the dictatorship, where he gathered information about the torture of fellow prisoners. His action was met with broad public attention, not least through the pictures of his arrest broadcasted on TV.

Through pictures and reports of German observers, investigative media research contributed to substantiating claims of Greek migrants. References to Germany's Nazi past served as an emotional bridge, which particularly mobilised the Left.

Exposure of torture: Amnesty International

Particularly Amnesty International contributed to discrediting the Greek dictatorship as a torture state. Prior to the putsch, the NGO founded in London in 1961 had only supported individual long-term prisoners in Greece.[51] Now the country became a new main field of operation. In late 1967, the NGO sent the American James Becket and the British lawyer and co-founder of Amnesty International, Anthony Marreco, to Athens for four weeks to do research. Both men met representatives of the Greek Foreign Office and politically persecuted persons several times, but they were not allowed to attend trials or visit the prison islands. They published a report in late January 1968 mentioning 2,777 political prisoners incarcerated without sentence. But even more important were the interviews with 16 tortured persons and statements of further 32 victims known by name. The report published in Strasbourg described with unprecedented candour how prisoners were arrested without trial and brutally abused. Beatings during the interrogations were often followed by foot whipping, after which the prisoners were forced to walk. Alongside electric shocks and pulling out fingernails, the report described that women were tortured vaginally and men through anal and testicular means. One could hear their screams in the cells, often filled with water.[52] Statements like these made Greece appear as a sadistic and violent regime similar to fascist torture states.

The Amnesty report was immediately circulated within the public of Western Europe. Even conservative newspapers, television channels and university groups spread it in Western states, and German Amnesty groups sent it to senior politicians.[53] Amnesty International also presented it to the Council of Europe, which put more international pressure on Greece. Because Amnesty had a reputation as a nonpartisan organisation and its report did not condemn the regime as such but factually described the fate of individual prisoners, it was met with more credibility than general statements of exiles and political groups. Especially the individual fate of the torture victims mobilised the public. In the United States the torture campaign resulted in public and congressional protests, whereon the government responded with certain restrictions.[54]

The Greek government condemned the Amnesty report as fictional and not verifiable because it did not reveal any names. With great confidence the regime in March 1968 invited Amnesty to visit Greece again and inspect any prison at its discretion. Indeed, the Amnesty activist was able to speak to 12 prisoners in detention centres of his own choosing. Nine of them risked making statements regarding their tortures, as a second report that contained the names of the tortured persons stated.[55] Thus the Colonels failed to impress Amnesty, and the torture claims were corroborated. A second attempt to refute the accusations of torture in the public show trials during July 1968 also failed: contrary to expectations, the tortured prisoners dared to make statements in court about their abuses. In order to compensate the loss of reputation the Colonels released many political prisoners.[56] After further research, the Amnesty activist Becket in 1970 published a book that contained the names of 426 torture victims, 126 places of torture and detailed individual reports, which substantiated that these were not anonymous, non-verifiable individual cases.[57]

In 1968, the Federal Chancellery already assigned the foreign intelligence service, the *Bundesnachrichtendienst* (BND), to investigate the Amnesty report on "alleged torture". In early 1969, the BND broadly confirmed the torture claims for the initial phase and "with some reservations" regarding the methods.[58] This appeared to internally prove the torture claims but rather deemed them individual cases during a transitional stage that had been overcome.[59]

The interplay of local Amnesty groups and transregional campaigns kept public awareness of the arrests in Greece alive. Many German Amnesty groups looked after one "adopted" Greek prisoner each, several dozens in total. They researched the inmates' fate and wrote numerous letters to West German and Greek politicians and celebrities, demanding their release.[60] In addition, the West German branch of Amnesty founded a "Griechenland-Spezialgruppe" (Greece Special Group) that provided material to the central London office, supporting its research activities on the ground. Prior to diplomatic meetings, for instance the planned visit of Federal Foreign Minister Scheel to Athens, Amnesty provided the politicians with detailed information about political prisoners.[61] Individual German Amnesty members also travelled to Greece to conduct further research and attend trials, and journalists who accompanied them brought coverage of these stories on television.[62]

In addition to information stalls in city centres, fundraising for persecuted people and vigils, Amnesty also made use of the pop culture. For instance, it planned to produce a record with the singer Mikis Theodorakis and accompanied his tour through West Germany with stalls providing information on the situation in Greece.[63] From 1968 onwards, several members of parliament, clerics and scientists inquired addresses and assessments of political prisoners from Amnesty International because the NGO was considered a trustworthy and nonpartisan source of information.[64] This way even regional Amnesty activists acquired knowledge that the West German embassy, politicians and intelligence services did not have or want to acquire. Amnesty's reports indicate that their "adopted" Greek prisoners were in fact released more frequently than others.[65] In doing so, Amnesty bolstered the fight against the dictatorship, which in return made Amnesty a visible organisation that was able to influence political decisions.

A radio station for oppositional migrants?
The Deutsche Welle

Radio programmes in the Greek language broadcasted by the *Bayerische Rundfunk* and the *Deutsche Welle* played a key role in mobilising the public. The *Bayerische Rundfunk*, a regional public radio and television channel located in Bavaria, already broadcasted a Greek programme from 1964 onwards to inform the growing number of migrant workers in West Germany and keep them away from communist programmes of the GDR.[66] With the consolidation of the dictatorship, reports on the violation of human rights increased. The liberal-conservative producer Pavlos Bakoyannis broadcasted critical commentaries on Saturdays that he often spoke himself. These were then aired in Greece by the *Deutsche Welle*. Bakoyannis hoped that as a result his fellow countrymen and -women "when returning to Greece will be a core group of people who know how a democratic society looks like".[67] The radio programmes were a voice of resistance in Germany.

Not only the Greek embassy and its consulate in Munich pressed for his dismissal. The production director of the *Bayerische Rundfunk* refused to do so, pointing out that with the Greek dictatorship "the spirit of Adolf Hitler" had been resurrected.[68] The Federal government also urged the *Bayerische Rundfunk* to stop Greek journalists from criticising the junta because otherwise Greece would broadcast its own programmes for Germany from Luxembourg. In 1969, the Foreign Office summoned the production director and emphasised that it was not in the German interest to "transfer domestic disputes of foreign countries to the Federal Republic".[69] This sounded as if a domestic Greek controversy were at stake here – rather than dictatorship and torture. A Foreign Office's meeting script from the following year insisted that "the commentaries in Greek language in their current form are contrary to our foreign political interests".[70] A false report on the allegedly devaluation of the Greek currency broadcasted in 1971 provided welcome leverage to restructure the programme. On 2 April 1971 the State Secretary of Foreign Affairs, Paul Frank, wrote to the artistic director of the *Bayerische Rundfunk* that the programme had harmed major West German business contracts.[71]

Foreign Minister Walter Scheel was finally successful in urging the Bavarian Minister President, Alfons Goppel (CSU), to change the Greek programme because otherwise Greece would introduce economic sanctions against the Federal Republic. From now on the director Walter von Cube was responsible for the programme. Bakoyannis's broadcasts on Saturdays were replaced by an international press review and finally by alternating commentaries.[72] However, Bakoyannis remained a leading critical voice against the Greek dictatorship.[73] Other critics still appeared on the programme. The example clearly illustrates that the government of the Federal Republic vehemently interfered in independent public service broadcasting in order to curb criticism of the dictatorship for the protection of foreign political and economic cooperation with Greece.

Even more major conflicts emerged with the Greek-language programmes of the *Deutsche Welle*, a public state-owned international broadcaster, because they were also aired in Greece. Financed by federal funds, the *Deutsche Welle* broadcasted in 34 languages all over the world at that time. Because it was meant to bolster the fight against communism, its programmes in the Russian language criticised the situation in the Soviet Union, while their broadcasts in Czech supported the opposition of the Prague Spring in 1968.[74] The Greek programmes, produced and spoken by migrants, already began in 1964. They were intended to strengthen the connections of migrant workers who returned to their home country with the Federal Republic and expand West German cultural diplomacy. Immediately after the putsch, the Foreign Office considered the *Deutsche Welle* as a tool to foster "Greece's return to the rule of law" without taking a stance itself.[75] Initially the half-hour long broadcasts did not attract much attention. Walter Steigner, a conservative Social Democrat who became artistic director in 1968, extended the programme. From then on, its four permanent editors and three freelance staff were all Greek who distanced themselves from the Regime of Colonels.[76] Two of them even supported the armed struggle against the dictatorship.[77] From 1969 the broadcasts became a strong voice against the regime. They were aired at a more audience-friendly time at 9:40 pm daily for an entire hour, which the broadcaster officially justified with the need to "maintain contact" with the approximately 200,000 Greek migrants who had returned to Greece. In addition, it pointed out that there was an interest in news "that were not spread by official news sources" and that the "countries of the Eastern Bloc" had expanded their programmes aired in Greece.[78] Thus, anti-communism justified a radio programme against an anti-communist dictatorship. The programme contained press reviews, interviews and commentaries. Alongside the editors of the *Deutsche Welle*, prominent exiles appeared on the programme such as the law professor Dimitris Tsatsos. Some of the journalists, like Kostas Nikolaou, were more radical critics so that the producer and the editor-in-chief had to permanently balance what was acceptable.[79]

From summer 1969 criticism in Greece was growing. The Athens newspaper *Nea Politeia*, which was close to the government, suggested the *Deutsche Welle* would broadcast "lying and offensive programmes" and the exile politicians Mitsotakis and Apostolakos were the driving force behind it.[80] Subsequently, the Greek government submitted complaints on a regular basis and tried a few times to impede reception with jamming transmitters. Due to the Greek interventions, the West German Foreign Office already demanded in the Broadcasting Council on 13 June 1969 "to substantially reduce criticism of the events in Greece" and not to play "the democratic schoolmaster".[81] The Greek embassy in Bonn and its government, the West German embassy in Athens and the Bonn Foreign Office kept protesting against the critical broadcasts of the *Deutsche Welle* during the following years. As a result, the programmes were more closely controlled: from 1970, contributions in the Greek language had to be translated and released before airing, and the new producer of the programme, a German with Greek language skills, was appointed. The artistic director refused to release some commentaries, for example those prior to the national day or the 1973 referendum. He stopped the reading of listener letters as well as some commentaries, such as those of the dissident and political economist Mario Nikolinakos, and the airing of Greek contributions of the *Bayerische Rundfunk*. Kostas Nikolaou lost his job as editor after some of his contributions failed to be released.[82] Nevertheless, many broadcasts of the *Deutsche Welle* still denounced the political conditions in Greece.

Especially the West German ambassador in Athens, Peter Limbourg, objected to criticisms of the dictatorship. He argued the *Deutsche Welle*, in contrast to French, British and American world services, broadcasted "one-sided and negative programmes", using expressions such as dictatorship and tyranny. Limbourg claimed that it only aired statements of left-wing exile politicians of the opposition but none of the government and painted a one-sided, negative picture of the economy. The programmes, he continued, alienated bourgeois opposition groups in Greece and "burdened German-Greek relations".[83] In contrast, the broadcaster should include "news material provided by the Greek government".[84] To be sure, even then it was part of the journalistic trade to quote both sides. But it was indeed problematic to demand that even dictatorships should have equal opportunity to present their side of the story on radio. Towards the GDR, the Soviet Union or China, the Foreign Office was less forthcoming.

Under pressure from the Foreign Office, the artistic director of the *Deutsche Welle*, Walter Steigner, came to a secret informal agreement in July 1972 with the Greek government in order to curb criticism. At a meeting in Athens with the state secretary of the Greek Prime Minister, Byron Stamatopoulos, Steigner agreed on mitigating several concrete aspects of the political criticism broadcasted by *Deutsche Welle*. The secret agreement read: "As of 1 October, editorials of the *Deutsche Welle* will only use the term 'Greek government'" (instead of "dictatorship" etc.). The share of both perspectives on certain events, for example interviews with the ambassador, and the share of German topics were to increase. "The *Deutsche Welle* will rectify false reports immediately" and "The *Deutsche Welle* offers the Greek government the opportunity to submit statements to it, which will be aired by the broadcaster." Contributions in Greek language were "immediately to be placed at the disposal" of the Greek government.[85] Steigner publicly defended his visit to Athens and his allegedly continuous critical attitude while he internally ensured the ambassador to Athens that criticism would decline in future.[86] This agreement was in fact a massive concession to the Greek government *and* the German Foreign Office.

Actions followed the agreement. Immediately after the settlement, the *Deutsche Welle* invited the Greek ambassador for an interview with friendly questions previously agreed on.[87] Accordingly, even statements such as "democracy has a permanent residence in Greece" remained uncommented. The artistic director maintained a close and confidential relationship with the Greek state secretary and emphasised that he was "always willing to accept official statements of the Greek government against broadcasts of the *Deutsche Welle* and include them in our programme."[88] However, some inquiries for interviews or statements addressed to Greek government representatives remained unanswered.[89]

Of course, these measures could not resolve the conflicts over the Greek programmes because the Greek government and the Foreign Office still identified critical contents.[90] The Foreign Office, which eventually set up its own radio surveillance service that translated broadcasts for the suspicious ambassador, continued complaining that the *Deutsche Welle* still aired reports on arrests, the "political totalitarian regime" or announcements of protest demonstrations, despite being prohibited to do so.[91] Especially the newly appointed director of the Greece department, the West German Georg Heyer, repeatedly had to justify certain statements towards the artistic director, for instance that the Areopagus, the supreme court of Greece for civil and criminal law, showed "no independence in sentencing".[92]

Despite these numerous reprimands by the artistic director, the editor-in-chief und diplomatic representatives, the Greek programme remained an important critical voice. The continued complaints of the Greek government are indicative that its wishes for controlled and favourable reports could not be satisfied anyway. Overall, the limited power of the artistic director became visible, particularly because Greek exiles did not shy away from conflicts with the production director. At the same time, the artistic director had to be cautious not to be seen as the mouthpiece of the Greek government, all the more because his reprimands were increasingly met with public criticism.[93] After the end of the dictatorship, German media outlets accused him of having made a pact with the Colonels, which was corroborated by a critical account of the former employer Kostas Nikolaou.[94]

There is much evidence to suggest that many oppositional Greeks still regularly listened to the programmes of the *Deutsche Welle*, despite the restrictions imposed by its director. Oppositional newspapers often referred to these broadcasts,[95] and after the end of the dictatorship the broadcaster received numerous letters of appreciation from listeners.[96] A major survey among the audiences of the *Deutsche Welle* for Greece conducted in 1977 emphasised that listeners stuck with the broadcaster even after the end of the Regime of the Colonels and were very happy with it, although they had listened to its programmes more often during the dictatorship.[97] Thus, the *Deutsche Welle* contributed to enhancing the image of the Federal Republic in Greece after the occupation during the Second World War. Moreover, many Greek staff of the *Deutsche Welle* were considered leading figures of the opposition, who after the end of the dictatorship took up senior positions in Greece. Now the Foreign Office and the management of the *Deutsche Welle* even prided themselves upon the fact that the West German broadcaster had bolstered the fall of the dictatorship and the opposition. And yet, as a matter of fact, the programmes had helped Greek migrants and West German editors take a stance against the dictatorship *despite* diplomatic interferences and interventions.

Conclusion

The chapter has shown to what extent the protests against Greek dictatorship in Federal Germany were driven and supported by Greek migrants. Together with parts of the New Left, investigative journalists, Amnesty International, trade unions and Social Democrats, they fostered a mobilisation directed against a non-communist dictatorship to a hitherto unprecedented extent in the Federal Republic. Frequent references to National Socialism were the justification for interventions in Greece's sovereignty. Moreover, the Left considered Greece an epitome of the threat to democracy in the Federal Republic and a seemingly looming new fascism in Europe. The manifold support of the Greek opposition, however, helped remedy the image of West Germans after the violence of the Second World War.

The West German government and particularly the Foreign Office made several attempts to suppress civil protests and media reports in order to not jeopardise economic relations with Greece. Nevertheless, the protests had a profound impact on politics. They played a part in contributing to cancelled state visits, reduced EEC funds and military aid and the specific support of the Greek opposition. Unlike the Scandinavian states and the Netherlands, the government of the Federal Republic did not take a critical stance but advocated what was at least a position of compromise in the Council of Europe.

The various protests can be seen as a milestone in the Federal Republic's debate on human rights. The thrive of Amnesty International, critical media reports and civil protests emphasised that the logic of the Cold War had been overcome and that no longer only victims of socialism were supported. Although the term human rights was seldom used as a universal concept, at stake here was also gathering broad open support for universal rights even for persecuted communists. In this sense, a solidarity movement emerged on which subsequent movements in the 1970s could draw.

Translated from German into English by Christine Brocks

---

[1] Cf. Mogens Pelt, *Tying Greece to the West: US-West German-Greek Relations 1949–1974* (Copenhagen: Museum Tusculanum, 2006), 345; Dimitris K. Apostopoulos, "Die deutsch-griechischen Wirtschaftsbeziehungen in der Nachkriegszeit," in: Wolfgang Schultheiss/Evangelos Chrysos (ed.) *Meilensteine deutsch-griechischer Beziehungen* (Berlin: Lit, 2010), 275–290.

[2] Cf. on the debate about the 1970s caesura: Samuel Moyn, *The Last Utopia. Human Rights in History* (Cambridge: Harvard University Press, 2010); Jan Eckel, *Die Ambivalenz des Guten: Menschenrechte in der in-*

ternationalen Politik seit den 1940ern (Göttingen: Vandenhoeck & Ruprecht, 2014).

3   On the diplomatic level cf. in addition to Pelt, *Tying*, for example Philipp Rock, *Macht und Moral. Märkte und Moral: zur Rolle der Menschenrechte in der Außenpolitik der Bundesrepublik Deutschland in den sechziger und siebziger Jahren* (Frankfurt a. M.: Peter Lang, 2010), 45–119.

4   Cf. in addition to the database of the Statistische Bundesamt, Christoph A. Rass, "Das Anwerbeabkommen der BRD mit Griechenland und Spanien im Kontext des europäischen Migrationssystems," in: Jochen Oltmer/Axel Kreienbrink/Carlos Sanz Díaz (eds.), *Das "Gastarbeiter"-System. Arbeitsmigration und ihre Folgen in der Bundesrepublik Deutschland* (Munich: Oldenbourg, 2012), 62–3. Unfortunately without discussing the period of dictatorship Eleni Tseligka, *From Gastarbeiter to European Expatriates. Greek Migrant Communities in Germany and their Socio-political Integration* (Frankfurt a. M.: Peter Lang, 2020).

5   From an international perspective: Kim Christiaens: "'Communists are no beasts'. European Solidarity Campaigns on Behalf of Democracy and Human Rights in Greece and East-West Détente in the 1960s and Early 1970s," in: *Contemporary European History* vol. 26 (2017) no. 4, 621–646.

6   On the organisations: Eberhard Rondholz, "Die Junta und die Deutschen. Zwischen Realpolitik und Solidarität. Eine Bilanz 50 Jahre nach dem Putsch," in: *Hellenika* 12 (2017), 20–47, here 23–4.

7   Cf. Alexander Clarkson, *Fragmented Fatherland: Immigration and Cold War Conflict in the Federal Republic of Germany, 1945–1980* (New York: Berghahn, 2013), 123, 132, 139.

8   In Stuttgart on 12 December 1969 according to: Thomas Paul Becker/Ute Schröder, *Die Studentenproteste der 60er Jahre: Archivführer, Chronik, Bibliographie* (Cologne: Böhlau, 2000), 276.

9   Becker/Schröder, *Die Studentenproteste*, 133–4, 205; Horst-Pierre Bothien, *Protest und Provokation: Bonner Studenten 1967/1968* (Essen: Klartext, 2007), 41.

10 For instance on 15 January 1968, cf. Becker/Schröder, *Die Studentenproteste*, 135, 167.

11 Cf. the posters of the exhibition: *Solidarität und Widerstand. Deutsch-griechische Beziehungen während der griechischen Militärdiktatur 1967–1974* (Bonn, 2017).

12 On the arrests: Kostis Kornetis, *Children of the Dictatorship. Student Resistance, Cultural Politics, and the "long 1960s" in Greece* (New York: Berghahn, 2013), 37–94.

13 According to the chronological table in: Becker/Schröder, *Die Studentenproteste*, 135.

14 Ibid., 151, 158: 2 September 1967 in Stuttgart, 17 November 1968 in Berlin.

15 Cf. video in: ARD Panorama 23 October 1967, 4:30–5:30. https://daserste.ndr.de/panorama/archiv/1967/panorama3893.html.

16 On 27 November 1967 according to: Becker/Schröder, *Die Studentenproteste*, 160.

17 Kornetēs, *Children*, 60–70.

18 8 July 1968, according to: Becker/Schröder, *Die Studentenproteste*, 205.

19 Internal meeting of the CDU parliamentary group on 28 June 1967, 3, in http://fraktionsprotokolle.de (last access 3 November 2022).

20 Sarah B. Snyder, "US human rights activism and the 1967 coup," in: Antonio Klapsis et al. (eds.), *The Greek Junta and the International System. A Case Study of Southern European Dictatorships, 1967–1974* (New York: Routledge, 2020), 137–149, here 140.

21 Tsiropoulos to Lord Mayor of Hamburg, 16 December 1969, Bundesarchiv Koblenz [BArch/K] B136/3629. "Schwarze Listen für Athen," *Die Zeit* No. 45. 7 November 1969; Bundestag 1 February 1973, 436 f.

22 The Federal Republic issued 500 non-German passports until 1973; Statistiken, BArch/K B 106/60283.

23 Cf. for example Prof. Wengler to Ehmke 1 December 1969, BArch/K B136/3629. On Tsatkos cf. B 136/6253.

24 To Heinemann 25 October 1972, BArch/K B 122/12672.

25 Diary entry 18 October 1969, Hans Werner Richter, *Mittendrin. Tagebücher 1966–1972* (Munich: Beck, 2012), 136.
26 According to contemporary witnesses 30 % (Basil Mathiopoulos: *Athen brennt. Der 21. April 1967 in Griechenland* (Darmstadt: Schneekluth, 1967), 218. Even half of it argues: Ilias Katsoulis, "Demokraten gegen Obristen. Griechen in Deutschland 1967–1974," in: Schultheiss/Chrysos *Meilensteine*, 291–98, here 295.
27 Rock, *Macht*, 49.
28 1968, BArch/K B 136/3629.
29 Mathiopoulos, *Athen brennt*, 217.
30 Metall-Pressedienst 28 December 1970, BArch/K B 136/6253.
31 Internal meeting of the SPD parliamentary group on 9 May 1967, 2–3, 27 June 1967, 6, in: http://fraktionsprotokolle.de (last access 3 November 2022).
32 Motion Helmut Schmidt for the SPD parliamentary group, Bundestag 29 June 1967, Drucksache V/1989.
33 Party conference of the Social Democratic Party of Germany, 17–21 March 1968 in Nuremberg. Minutes of the Proceedings, Bonn 1968, 1071.
34 Cf. the questions by Felder, Blachstein, Schulz and Matthöfer, in: Bundestag 4 October 1967, 6121–3.
35 Boss to Undersecretary 26 April 1968, BArch/K B 136/3629.
36 Cf. Rock, *Macht*, 66–9.
37 Paul Frank, *Entschlüsselte Botschaft – Ein Diplomat macht Inventur* (Stuttgart: Deutsche Verlags-Anstalt, 1981), 226–7; cf. Mathiopoulos, *Athen brennt*, 113–4, 128–38.
38 Cf. ibid.; cf. for example: Basil Mathiopoulos, "Griechenland zehn Wochen nach dem Militärputsch: Die Obristen werden unsicher," *Sozialdemokratischer Pressedienst*, 27 June 1967, 3–4.
39 "Pattakos scherzt über Verhaftungen," *FAZ* 30 May 1967, 3.
40 Cf. "Griechenland. Insel des Teufels," *Spiegel* 24 July 1967, 82–3; "Bei Ankunft auf der griechischen KZ-Insel Jaros," *Spiegel* 31 July 1966, 16.
41 "Die Insel der Verbannten," *Stern* 6 August 1967, 16–23. Cf. also Joachim Seyppel, *Hellas Geburt einer Tyrannis. Impressionen, Analysen, Dokumente* (Berlin: Blanvalet, 1968).
42 Without exact figures Michalis Nikolakakis, "The Colonels on the Beach: Tourism Policy During the Greek Military Dictatorship (1967–1974)," in: *Journal of Modern Greek Studies* 35.2 (2017), 425–50, here 444.
43 Janis Nalbadidacis, *Geburtshelfer der Demokratie. Die Militärdiktatur in Griechenland, 1967–1974*, in: Jörg Ganzenmüller (ed.), *Europas vergessene Diktaturen? Diktatur und Diktaturüberwindung in Spanien, Portugal und Griechenland* (Cologne: Böhlau, 2018), 91–110, here 100–3.
44 Prisoners of the Lakki-Laros concentration camp to Brandt 20 December 1969, BArch/K B 136/3629.
45 Clarkson, *Fragmented Fatherland*, 128.
46 "Arndt nicht ohne Hoffnung," *FAZ* 19 February 1968, 3.
47 Embassy Athens to Foreign Office 25 October 1971, BArch/K B 136/7116.
48 Embassy Athens to Foreign Office 26 January 1973, BArch/K B 136/7116. Cf. also "Griechenland: Schlammiger Fluß," *Spiegel* No. 5, 29 January 1973, 72.
49 Werner Robbers, "Freiheit gibt es nur im Gefängnis," *Die Zeit*, 9 February 1973, 7.
50 Cf. his self-portrayal Günter Wallraff/Eckart Spoo, *Unser Faschismus nebenan: Griechenland gestern – ein Lehrstück für morgen* (Cologne: Kiepenheuer & Witsch, 1975), 57, 187.
51 Amnesty International Annual report, 1 June 1966–31 May 1967.
52 Situation in Greece. Report by Amnesty International, 27 January 1968. These detailed torture reports were later published in: James Becket, *Barbarism in Greece. A young American lawyer's inquiry into the use of torture in contemporary Greece* (New York: Walker, 1970). Cf. on the background of Becket, whose wife was Greek: Konstantina Maragkou, "The Beckets vs. the Colonels. A

53 study in the micro-evolution of global human rights activism in the 'long 1960s'," in Klapsis, *The Greek Junta*, 149-63, here 151. On this briefly Tom Buchanan, *Amnesty International and Human Rights Activism in Postwar Britain, 1945-1977* (Cambridge: Cambridge University Press, 2020), 184-187.

53 Cf. for example report Amnesty Cologne 27 January 1968, BArch/K B 122 15 077; Thankmar von Münchhausen, "Sorge um politische Gefangene in Griechenland," *FAZ* 13 February 1968, 4. On the dissemination of 'Law Information' of the Cologne students, BArch/K B 136/3629.

54 Cf. Barbara Keys, "Anti-Torture Politics: Amnesty International, the Greek Junta, and the Origins of the U.S. Human Rights Boom," in: Akira Iriye et al. (eds.), *The Human Rights Revolution: An International History* (Oxford: Oxford University Press, 2012), 201-22.

55 Second Report Amnesty, 6 April 1968, BArch/K B 122 15 077; Amnesty International Annual Report, June 1967-May 1968, 6.

56 Heinz A. Richter, *Griechenland 1950-1974. Zwischen Demokratie und Diktatur* (Wiesbaden: Harrasowitz, 2013), 325.

57 Documents in Becket, *Barbarism*, 44-123, 210-242.

58 Head of the Federal Chancellery to BND, 4 February 1969 and BND to Head of Federal Chancellery 28 February 1969, BArch/K B 136/3629.

59 Department 1, 16 January 1969 and Head of Federal Chancellery to Hundhammer, 14 February 1969, BArch/K B 136/3629.

60 Cf. for example Amnesty Freiburg, Dossier zum Fall Konstantinos Voyatzakis, 6 April 1968, BArch/K B 122 15 077.

61 AI to Scheel, 6 March 1973, Archiv Amnesty Deutschland, Ordner Vorstandssitzungen 1972-1973.

62 Report Amnesty Freiburg, 18 April 1968 and excerpt ZDF Magazin, BArch/K B 122 15 077.

63 AI board meeting minutes, 25 November 1972 and AI board meeting minutes, 24/25 June 1972, Archiv Amnesty Deutschland, Ordner Vorstandssitzungen from 1968.

64 Correspondence from 1968 to 1970, BArch/K B 122 15 077.

65 52 released 'adopted' cases after 1 ½ years according to Amnesty International Annual Report, June 1968-May 1969, 6.

66 On the context of the 'Gastarbeiterprogramm' – a programme to recruit migrant workers mostly from Southern Europe to work in the Federal Republic – see Roberto Sala, *Fremde Worte. Medien für 'Gastarbeiter' in der Bundesrepublik im Spannungsfeld von Außen- und Sozialpolitik* (Paderborn: Schöningh, 2011), 94-5.

67 30 March 1968, quoted in Bayerischer Rundfunk (ed.), *Die Ausländerprogramme*, 49.

68 Nikos Papanastasiou, "The Bavarian Greek radio programme for Greek migrants and its impact on Greek-German relations, 1967-74," in: Klapsis, *The Greek Junta*, 58-70, here 61-63.

69 Script for parliamentary state secretary 28 February 1969, BArch/K B 145/6644.

70 According to script 20 July 1970 Foreign Office, quoted in Dimitrios Gounaris, *Die Geschichte der sozialliberalen Rüstungsexportpolitik. Ein Instrument der deutschen Außenpolitik 1969-1982* (Wiesbaden: Springer, 2019), 159.

71 Frank to Wallenreiter 2 April 1971, quoted in *Akten zur Auswärtigen Politik der Bundesrepublik Deutschland* [AAPD] *1971*, ed. Martin Koopmann, Matthias Peter, Daniela Taschler (Berlin: De Gruyter, 2014), 922, FN 17.

72 Papanastasiou, "The Bavarian Greek radio programme," 64

73 Pavlos Bakojannis, *Militärherrschaft in Griechenland. Eine Analyse zu Parakapitalismus und Spätfaschismus* (Stuttgart: Kohlhammer, 1972).

74 Anke Hagedorn, *Die Deutsche Welle und die Politik deutscher Auslandsrundfunk 1953-2013* (Konstanz: UVK, 2016), 291-296.

75 Note Böker/Foreign Office 24 August 1967, AAPD 1967, 1219-1222, here 1221.

76 Cf. overview 16 February 1973, BArch/K B 187/4162.
77 Cf. the contemporary witness reports of the Greek editors in the TV documentary: 'Wort und Widerstand 2009'.
78 'Nachkontakt auf kurzer Welle', DW *report* 3/69 and DW *report* 4/69.
79 Cf. for example Steigner to Drexelius/Schollwer [1972], BArch/K B 187/4160.
80 DW *report* 7/1969.
81 Hagedorn, *Die Deutsche Welle*, 331–3.
82 According to his critical autobiographical account from 1975, Kostas Nikolaou, "21:40–22:40 [Ώρα Ελλάδος: *21:40–22:40*. Αγνωστες Πτυχές της Ελληνικής Εκπομπής της "Ντώϋτσε Βέλλε"]" (Athens, 1975), BArch/K B 187/4162.
83 Limbourg/embassy Athens to Foreign Office, 10 May 1971, BArch/K B 136/3629, id. to Foreign Office 15 January 1971, AAPD 1971, 80.
84 Cf. Hagedorn, *Die Deutsche Welle*, 340.
85 Artistic director/Walter Steigner memory minutes of conversation with Stamatopoulos on 14 July 1972, BArch/K B 187/4160.
86 Ambassador Athens to Foreign Office, 10 July 1972, BArch/K B 136/6253. Anders, "Kein Zurückweichen vor der Junta," *Frankfurter Rundschau*, 18 July 1972.
87 Steigner to Botschafter Sionis, 8 August 1972 and manuscript of the broadcast, BArch/K B 187/4160. By emphasising the concessions I dissociate myself from Hagedorn, *Deutsche Welle*, and Fleischer, *Krieg*, 269.
88 Steigner to Stamatopoulos, 16 August 1972, BArch/K B 187/4160.
89 Heyer to Steigner, 30 August 1973, BArch/K B 187/4162.
90 Stamatopoulos to Steigner, 2 December 1972, BArch/K B 187/4160.
91 Memo, 17 May 1973, BArch/K B 187/4160.
92 Heyer to Steigner, 22 August 1973, BArch/K B 187/4162.
93 WDR1 on 30 November 1973; Steigner to Bismarck, 4 December 1973, BArch/K B 187/4162.
94 funk report 11/1975, 29 August 1975; Gong No. 25/1975. Nikolaou, *21:40–22:40*, BArch/K B 187/4162.
95 U. Pielsticker, "Deutsche Welle in Griechenland," DW *report* 4/1974, 26–7 and Schlegel/DW, 29 January 1974, BArch/K B 187/4162.
96 Heyer/DW *report*, September 1974, 25–6, BArch/K B 187/4162.
97 Heyer, "Die Deutsche Welle und ihre griechischen Hörer," DW *report* [undated, c. 1977/78], 18–20, Archiv Deutsche Welle.

Antonis Sarantidis

The Greek Students' Resistance against the Junta in Western Europe: The Case of European Student Conferences (1967–1971)

After the imposition of military rule through a coup d'etat in Greece in April 1967, a large wave of student migration abroad occurred. Specifically, the number of Greeks attending international universities increased from 9,375 students in 1966 to 22,587 in 1974, the countries of Western Europe, such as England, France, Italy and West Germany, being the main destinations for these student movements.[1] For instance, in West Germany the number of Greeks studying at the country's universities increased from 2.176 to 3.073 from 1967 to 1974. More than 600 Greek students were registered in the two university institutions of West Berlin, the Free University and the University Of Technology, where they respectively founded Greek student associations.[2]

The political and social situation in their homeland along with the persecution, the imprisonments and the tortures that their colleagues had been suffered in Greece, were central reasons to mobilize them against junta and often made them to strive for more cohesive actions. During the whole period of 1967–1974, Greek students and their official unions in Western European countries had a very active role in the anti-dictatorial movement abroad. They also experienced and were directly influenced by the international social and youth movements that flourished in the late '60s. Especially after May 1968, a general youth culture was formed that questioned everything related to the political, social and cultural status quo, and contributed to the composition of a "New Left", which expressed its opposition to any form of governmental totalitarianism and authoritarianism while also sharply criticizing the traditional Left.[3]

Through the activation of the existing unions, the publication of leaflets, the organization of protest events, press conferences and concerts, the Greek students abroad tried to inform and activate the international public opinion about the political situation in Greece throughout the dictatorship. At the same time, they collaborated with their foreign colleagues and actively participated in anti-imperialist demonstrations, taking part in events and marches in all the major campuses of Western Europe. So, within this context, how did Greek students abroad try to achieve unified coordination within the Greek student movement, while at the same time realigning the movement into a common anti-dictatorial direction? In this article, the efforts that were made for the unified coordination of the Greek student movement abroad will be presented, with the most characteristic examples being the European Conferences of Greek Students in Paris in 1967, in Lund in 1969 and in Copenhagen in 1971, which had a clear anti-dictatorial orientation.

The First European Conference of Greek Students Abroad (1967)

From the first days after the overthrow of democracy in Greece, the first thoughts began to be expressed by the administrations of some student associations abroad about the necessity of cooperation in the struggle against the regime. Therefore, the task of a European student conference would have to overcome the strategies of the past and express the anti-dictatorial spirit that pervaded the majority of students in Greece and abroad. As characteristically being noted in a relevant proclamation in April 1967, the forthcoming European student conference would "express the decision of the free Greeks to resist fascism".[4]

The first European Conference of Greek Students convened on

27–28 May 1967 in Paris, while the active Board of the Union of Greek Students in Paris (EPES) undertook the further organizational procedures.[5] Just one week after the imposition of the coup, members of the union visited Belgium, Germany, Austria and Italy to reach an agreement with the local Greek student unions and associations. They also went to Prague to contact the International Union of Students (I. U. S.), which agreed to support financially the effort.[6] Nicos Hadjinicolaou, a PhD student in Paris and president of EPES in the period 1966–1968, in his personal testimony to the writer, he described the coalescence network that was developed immediately after the coup and led to the organization of the conference. He underlined that

> "we immediately went to UNEF and they booked us air tickets. Alekos Giotopoulos and I went to Prague [...] at the headquarters of the I. U. S. [...] and then I went to Rome, where the Greek Students' Association had a big meeting [...] where on Easter [of 1967] I made my first acquaintances with Christos Kotoulas, Anna Filini, Giorgos Tsikouris. Angelos [Elephantis] went to London. So there was a readiness [...] and immediately this conference took place, which was something very important, for the future too".[7]

Representatives of Greek student federations and unions of thirteen European countries took part in the conference. The relevant documents emphasize the special importance of participating, for the first time in a Greek student conference as equal members, representatives of the student associations of the socialist countries, something that had not been achieved prior to the dictatorship.[8] Also, during the conference, many international student associations sent messages of support to the delegates, thus ensuring that the struggle of their Greek colleagues against the dictatorship was recognized throughout the international student community.[9] A Coordinating Committee of Greek Student Associations Abroad based in London was elected during the process, which was represented by a seven-member Executive Secretariat consisting of representatives from England, West and East Germany, Italy and Austria. A four-member committee of the National Student Association of Greece (E. F. E. E.) Abroad was also elected as a representative body in international relations with the participation of representatives from England, West Germany and Czechoslovakia.[10]

Presentations during the conference were made by the delegates from West Germany and Italy, while the main proposal was that of the representatives of France, which was unanimously adopted as the main resolution of the conference too. The participants' resolutions largely reflect the dialogue that had developed in the Greek student communities abroad since the pre-dictatorial period regarding the political and social situation in Greece. Also, although at an early stage, the significant impact that the coup had on the consciences of Greek students is highlighted, as well as a series of reference points that would later be the content of ideological consensus or conflicts within the Greek student movement abroad. Makis Kavouriaris, vice president of EPES at that time, estimates in an interview with the writer that

> "the first conference is important because it laid the foundations of a position that had not been consolidated. The Communist Party then, I believe, [...] had not expressed a clear view of where things were going and what we could do, especially at the level of alliances. [...] It spoke against the dictatorship, but nothing specific, there was a little hesitation. While we, in the First Congress, expressed that we were against the regime by all means, that the character of the dictatorship is a state of emergency, it is not a fascist dictatorship and it has no basis in the people".[11]

With the views expressed through the conference, it became clear that Greek students abroad aimed to claim a leading role in the anti-dictatorship struggle, listening to the demands of their foreign colleagues referring to the evolution of the new social movements that emerged in Western countries in the late '60s. Based on the decisions of the congress, it was a common finding that the anti-dictatorship struggle had to be leaded by ideological features that would express the unconditional opposition to the regime of the colonels. At the same time, an "anti-monarchist" aspect was attributed which indicated the criticism and disapproval of the policies and manipulations of the central government pre-dictatorially, but also an "anti-imperialist" aspect regarding the role of the foreign factor in imposing the coup, and specifically the role of USA.[12]

One of the underlined key points was the question of "unity" in the lines of the movement against the junta, especially between the progressive forces, an issue which would occupy the dialogue between anti-dictatorship organizations on several occasions until 1973. The central resolution of the conference emphasized on that "the struggle, that is now beginning, requires the unity of all anti-dictatorial, anti-monarchist and anti-imperialist forces. All Greek students are invited to contribute to the real accomplishment of this unity".[13] This point was made at a time when the youth organizations of the Greek Left and Centre abroad were in an incipient stage of restructuring their forces after the shock of the coup. Just a few days earlier in May 1967, the anti-dictatorial organizations of Patriotic Anti-dictatorial Front (P. A. M.) and Democratic Defense had made their founding declarations.[14]

Of particular interest is the position given in the central resolution regarding the practices of the anti-dictatorship struggle in Greece and abroad, especially the reference to more dynamic actions against the regime in case they would be necessary. This finding indicates that the references to "armed response" and "immediate action", which in the coming years would be a topic in the wider dialogue developed within the anti-dictatorship circles, already existed within the Greek student movement abroad. Apparently, the decisions of the conference had a third dimension that was associated with the day after the fall of the dictatorship. It is emphasized that "at the end of this struggle the Greek people will decide freely about their future. To this end, an interim government will be formed consisting of all the parties and forces that will have fought against the dictatorship".[15] These optimistic views were based on initial assessments of the temporary nature of the dictatorship and the lack of factors that would contribute to its consolidation in Greek society through the creation of any social base. Of course, the degree of resilience that the regime would subsequently develop had not been assessed yet.[16]

During the conference but also in its immediate aftermath, there was no lack of ideological controversies or criticisms regarding the general orientation of the conference. The election of E. F. E. E. Abroad, as official representative of the then illegal E. F. E. E. in Greece, was accompanied by a series of negative reactions. The representatives from Italy did not participate in the four-member committee, while the proposal was also voted against by the delegates of France. At the center of the difference was the decision as to whether this committee would have the legal basis to represent the Greek Union EFEE in international student bodies, especially at a time when the latter was completely disorganized. In contrast, the plenary session of Greek student unions abroad was judged as the fairest way of representation, at least until the appropriate conditions could be created in Greece for the E. F. E. E. itself to take initiatives and decisions in this direction.[17]

The issues of the way of representation in the next conferences created equally frictions between the participants. In this case, the main focus of the controversy was whether the representatives at the conferences and the members of the coordinating committee had to come from the administrations of the Greek student federations, such as the Federations of Greek Students' Unions in West Germany and Italy, or directly from the administrations of the Greek student unions of each country. The representatives of Italy, contrary to the general spirit of the conference which focused on the role of the federations, proposed that the delegates of the student unions abroad, as direct mediators of the Greek student movement, must be considered as the only lever for the convening of the next European conferences and also for the structuring of the coordinating committees in the future. These proposals were again supported by the representatives of France. The different positions during the conference, although they did not create an open ideological division between the warring groups, showed that the representatives of the Greek student communities were looking for the framework that would carve out a new identity for themselves through organizational reforms, which in that point had to balance between the past and the present. On the one hand, a unifying line between the Left, the Center and the other democratic forces had to be a clear target for the Greek student movement, as it was during the pre-dictatorial period, in order to express the opposition to the Junta's regime. On the other hand, the form of representation that had been established before 1967, focused on the student federations and not on the student unions, was no longer fully accepted by the student circles abroad.[18]

Taking into consideration that in the period of the imposition of the coup in Greece most of the politically active Greek students abroad were members of the youth organizations of the Left, like the United Democratic Left (E. D. A.) and the Communist Party, no divergence from the official line was formalized during the conference since the activity of the pre-dictatorial parties of the Left or the Center was defined as the main orientation of the students' anti-dictatorship action. However, the emergence of the first anti-dictatorial organizations within the country was put into the equation as factor for the development of the anti-dictatorship movement and the coordination of the student unions abroad. In this context, the attitude of the representatives of France and Italy towards the issue of associations, which mainly expressed the line of the political leadership of the E. D. A. and Centre Union, could be seen as a slight on the higher echelons who tried to oversee the procedures of the conference. As confirmed by a subsequent report by the Student Union in Paris administration, in which E. D. A. had a majority in 1967, its delegates refused to participate in the elected secretariat because they considered its final structure "ineffective".[19] In addition, Greek leftist organizations published soon after proclamations strongly criticizing the terms and general guidelines of the European conference.[20]

Another issue that provoked intense discussions among the representatives was the statements on the likelihood and legitimacy of dynamic resistance against junta. The idea of embracing violent means of resistance created ambiguity, especially among the leaders of the political youth organizations who distanced themselves from this perspective. Venios Angelopoulos, a student in Paris and member of the student union there, later testified that "we had a significant rift between the base and the leadership of the Greek Left", and added that "at the conference we realized that […] if the leadership of the movement had not yet fallen, it had proved to be insufficient at least".[21]

One day after the closure of the conference, a student organization was formally established in Paris, called the 'Movement of the 29th May'. This new organization unequivocally criticized the attitude of the majority of delegates as damaging the reputation of their movement and feared that the "necessary use of violent means" would be elevated to the status of a fundamental principle in the anti-dictatorial struggle in Greece.[22] These attitudes created confusion in the leading ranks of Greek Left abroad because discerned tendencies of autonomy in student initiatives. Possibly, this was the reason the conference was completely ignored by the official anti-dictatorial publications and announcements of Left in the next two years.[23]

The Conferences of Lund (1969) and Copenhagen (1971)

On the one hand, the Paris conference laid the foundations for a unified coordinating framework for Greek students in Europe, it facilitated the development of networks between them, and it was presented as a legal tool of the dynamic role sought by the student movement in the anti-dictatorship struggle. On the other hand, the conceptual complexity of a military coup in their homeland and the need for the convening of the congress in a very short time after the imposition of the dictatorship, left important issues open in terms of goals and general orientation of the student movement abroad.[24]

Until the next student conference, which took place two years later, the new developments, which occurred in Greece, would be decisive for the evolution of the anti-dictatorial movement. The split of the Greek Communist Party in February 1968 sealed "dualism" that existed within it and in the grassroots organizations and it intensified the ideological disputes in the assemblies of the Greek associations abroad between the members of the respective "exterior" and "interior" factions.[25] Furthermore, the invasion of Czechoslovakia by the Soviet troops in August of that year, apart from the sealing of the Communist Party split, wiped out any possibility of an ideological compromise between the political factions and among student organizations, which added to a wider climate of intense conflict about claiming the communist heritage.[26] In Greece, the regime's feigned attempts at "liberalization" with the illegitimately held referendum on the autocratic "constitution" of 1968, the coup attempt by King Constantine II and the erratic moves of the junta leadership in the international discussions preceding Greece's expulsion from the Council of Europe in 1969,[27] motivated Greek students abroad to further expand their anti-dictatorship activities. Even more crucial was the increase in the number of anti-dictatorial organizations until 1968, as well as the numerous persecutions and trials of activists and students by the junta until 1969,[28] which intensified the aspirations of Greek students for a more coordinated action at a European level in order to strengthen the struggle of their colleagues in Greece.

The 2nd European Conference of Greek Students Abroad was convened on 27–30 June 1969 in Lund, Sweden. Representatives of the federations of West Germany and Italy took part and also the student unions of East Germany, Geneva, London, Paris, Graz, Vienna, Stockholm and Czechoslovakia. The main resolutions of the conference came from the representatives of England and France. The general orientation of the conference emerges in its first and central resolution, which also summarizes the redefinition of the reference points of a large portion of the Greek student abroad, and mainly on the Left. The anti-fascist, anti-imperialist element remained the dominant ideological line, while the dictatorship continued to be interpreted as "a consequence of the development and intensification of contradictions in post-war Greece, a consequence in the impasse of the ruling class and its foreign allies". At this point, however, the departure from some of the findings of the Paris conference became apparent, as it was clearly emphasized that the junta was also a consequence of "the inability of the progressive movement to form an appropriate tactic despite the rising of class consciousness in large parts of the Greek population".[29]

This dimension highlights the lack of trust expressed by student circles abroad, coming mainly from the Communist Party (Int.) but also the leftist organizations that gradually made their presence much more dynamic, towards the pre-dictatorial parties such as E. D. A., Communist Party and Centre Union. The main point of criticism was that the progressive political parties were insufficiently prepared for the overthrow of democracy. In addition, many of the delegates in the second conference expressed the concern that the actions of the anti-dictatorship movement's leadership against the junta had been ineffective.[30] According to the main resolution of the conference in Lund, the center of gravity for the evolution of the anti-dictatorship struggle inside the country and the wider social and political change that was sought before the dictatorship, was estimated by the majority of the conference's participants to be the anti-dictatorial organizations which were now active in Western Europe too, such as P. A. M., Democratic Defense, P. A. K., and especially their youth organizations operating in Greece, like 'Rigas Ferraios' and the student section of the Democratic Defense.[31]

Nevertheless, the turn taking place at the Lund congress did not amount to a rupture with the leadership of the parties of the Left. In fact, many of the Greek students remained members of political youth collectives and at the same time joined the respective anti-dictatorship organizations. In practice, it was a crystallization of the original formulations of the First Congress, according to which the Greek student movement had to transform its previous orientation, which was based on pre-dictatorial frameworks, and to adopt a modern and more independent character, keeping pace with the general zeitgeist when the international student movement was emerging as a new collective and revolutionary subject.[32]

At the same time, an attempt was made to update an element of the identity of the Greek student movement abroad, which gradually emerged from the early 1960s but was violently opposed by the enforcement of the coup. This element lies in the fact that Greek students at home and abroad, despite any differences that arise from country to country, were part of a single Greek student movement with common perspectives and aspirations. The key form of representation of the Greek student movement as a whole had to be, on the one hand, the youth anti-dictatorship organizations in Greece, and on the other hand the Greek student unions in the European campuses.[33]

This position set the conditions for the next European conference, announced at the end of the Lund conference. In particular, it was decided that in the body elected for international relations would now participate equally the representatives of the student anti-dictatorship organizations, which would also be the links between the resistance organizations in Greece and the student unions abroad. At the same time, the role of the Greek student federations of Germany and Italy was greatly minimized, since the unions were now identified as the only bodies representing the local student communities.[34]

The Third European Conference was convened in Copenhagen on

20–22 January 1971 and was the largest in terms of participation, with 71 delegates and observers from Western and Eastern Europe.[35] For the first time, representatives of the student sections of the anti-dictatorial organizations officially participated. Finally, a new 3-member representative body of the E. F. E. E. Abroad was elected, which would be responsible for international relations, with two members from Paris and one from Geneva.[36] It is characteristic that only elected representatives of the student unions took part in the proceedings and not representatives of the student federations of West Germany and Italy, as was done in the two previous conferences. A statement from the EFEE International Relations Committee in September 1970 emphasized that "representatives of the Federations are entitled to attend the Conference, but without the right to vote".[37] This fact, besides the confirmation of the decisions and the general orientation of the Lund's conference, also confirmed the predictions by members of many Greek student unions abroad that the climate in the planned third European conference would be particularly factional and tense.[38]

These concerns connected to the wider debate that arose in the period of 1969–1971 among Greek students in Western Europe regarding the level of mobilization of anti-dictatorship forces in Greek communities. Although the anti-dictatorial student movement had been very active during this period, one of the main demands, which was to further expand the influence and the effectiveness of the unions in order to be reduced to the most decisive factor of the anti-dictatorship movement abroad, had not yet reached the desired results. On the one hand, the junta's intimidation tactics against Greek students through its embassies and local supporters proved a deterrent to the mass expansion of associations and unions. On the other hand, the eruption of the ideological conflicts between the factions of the traditional Left in the context of the elaborations of the Greek student collectives, especially in France, West Germany and Italy, had escalated into an intellectual warfare which in some cases prevented the active integration of students and obstructed the operation of the unions.[39]

As expected, the escalation of this conflict between the supporters of the Communist Party and the Communist Party (Int.) was transferred to the procedures of the Copenhagen conference. As for the central resolution of the conference, a proposal of the Student Union of Paris, in which the Communist Party (Int.) had a majority until that point, focused more on the anti-imperialist and anti-monopoly character of the anti-dictatorial movement in Greece and abroad. The resolution concludes with the general finding that "it is therefore the duty of the student movement abroad to develop the anti-dictatorship action of Greek students abroad and to help all student resistance organizations with the aim of violently overthrowing the regime in Greece".[40] On the third and final day of the conference, during the election of the new three-member coordinating committee and after two days of intense ideological controversy between the delegates of the unions, the works of the last sessions was the reason for the manifestation of the rupture. It is indicative that the line of Communist Party (Int.) supporters prevailed with the majority of delegates but in many of the resolutions and in the election process of the new E. F . E . E. committee, the Communist Party supporters left while the members of Centre Union and P . A . K. took basically a neutral stance in the conflict.[41]

The Copenhagen conference left a negative impression on student circles, and revealed that the effort for a European unified coordination was at a standstill. Dimitris Vlantos, a student at the Technical University of Hamburg at the time and president of the local Greek student union in 1972, in an interview with the author conveyed the repercussions left by the conferences on members of the student community in West Germany, underlining that "although I did not have direct experience from the conferences, what I know is that everything was crowned with a failure of understanding due to the intense political confrontation". Regarding the issue of broader coordination, he adds that "this was difficult to be done at the local level, in Hamburg or Berlin, all the more so at the federal level or more broadly, where you measured political power and influence".[42] Members of the Greek Communist Party youth organizations in the European cities complained to the organizing committee of the conference that it was trying to monopolize the process and decisions of the conference by interrupting or excluding opposing positions and not allowing for substantive representation. At the same time, they expressed their disagreement with the general ideological orientation of the current and previous conferences, regarding the points of reference of the student movement abroad and the anti-dictatorship struggle in general, the perspective of the "armed resistance" and the creation of a "controversial" representative body of the E. F. E. E.[43]

Conversely, the newspapers close to the Communist Party (Int.) harshly criticized the strategy of the Communist Party members during the conference. In the *Poreia*, which was the official publication of the Paris student union, it was pointed out that these actions led to nothing more than "dragging us into a sterile war (which in fact does not lead to an ideological strengthening of the student movement through criticism, but at its systematic deterioration)".[44] In *Eleftheri Ellada*, published in Rome, an article mentions "pre-planned divisive action of this group which hindered from the first moment the smooth prosecution of the conference" and that "the divisive group seeks and prepares formalization of the division also in the student space at an international level".[45] In *Eleftheri Patrida*, it is pointed out that the "divisive tactics" of the Communist Party members were transferred after the conference to the works of Greek student associations in Western Europe, which highlights the fact that the conflict between the youth organizations of the traditional Left had reached a tipping point in 1971 and that the Copenhagen conference had a significant impact on its further escalation.[46]

It would not be unreasonable to assume that the escalation of these conflicts between the student groups of the traditional Left translated into the reduction of their influence on the student unions of Western Europe. In parallel with the above escalation, the aftermath of May '68 and the emergence of the New Left ideas, the reduced effectiveness of the anti-dictatorship struggle inside Greece and the unsuccessful efforts of the anti-dictatorial forces to achieve a solid program of political alliances until that period, leftist student organizations significantly strengthened in many Western European countries, gradually gaining a majority in the assemblies of many student unions.[47] In England in 1971, the Union of Greek Student in London was substantially re-established under the administration of the *Socialist Student Faction*. In *Foititiki Protoporia,* the official publication of the union in London, the Trotskyist organization does not share any view on the autonomy of the student body from the labor movement and also on the coordination of Greek students abroad based on an organizational structure predetermined by unions' leaderships.[48]

The Maoist Fighting Front of Greeks Abroad (A. M. E. E.) which took over the management of the Greek student union in France and also of many unions in Italy since 1971,[49] published a 40-page pamphlet in February 1971 on which harshly criticizing all conferences, emphasizing on their "failure" on the organizational and practical level, accusing the supporters of the traditional Left parties of "revisionism" and that they had inactivated the student movement abroad with their practices, turning the collective student bodies into "seal associations".[50] In one of its relevant publications regarding the student movement abroad, A. A. S. P. E. (the Anti-Fascist Anti-Imperialist Student Faction Abroad), which had taken over the administration of the Greek Students' Union of West Berlin in 1972, makes absolutely no reference to the conferences.[51]

Conclusion

Several possible factors appear that did not favor the convening of a new European congress in the last three years of the dictatorship: the organizational deadlock and the ideological rift that escalated after the Copenhagen conference, reflected in the tilting balance of power among student unions towards Maoist and Trotskyist organizations since 1971, in combination with the events of the Polytechnic School in November 1973 in Greece which set the conditions for a massive student anti-dictatorship movement on the ground in Greece. The conferences in Paris, Lund and Copenhagen were a summary of the potential that the Greek student movement abroad had acquired during the period of 1967–1974 and broached new priorities that had arisen from the coup. The search for a unified coordinating framework, the development of multilevel networks abroad, the dialogue about the most effective forms of struggle and anti-dictatorial action, the promotion and the establishment of ideological schemes and inspirations, partly linked the conference initiatives with the element of self-determination of the Greek student movement abroad. Besides, suchlike elements characterized the international student movement as a whole.[52]

On the other hand, the exact same components highlighted the limits of these student initiatives, at least at the level of European coalescence. Differences at ideological and strategic levels, but also the different stimuli members of Greek student communities received from their respective host countries, made the task particularly difficult. These elements are not peculiar only to the Greek case, especially in the '60s and '70s. As Martin Klimke and Joachim Scharloth point out, referring to a broader context,

> "the many international contacts and meetings between European activists therefore did not always lead to tight and permanent networks transcending national borders but could equally showcase the dissent among activists triggered by the antagonisms of the Cold War".[53]

1. *Statistics of Students Abroad 1962–1968* (Paris: Unesco, 1972); *Statistics of Students Abroad 1969–1973* (Paris: Unesco, 1976); *Statistics of Students Abroad 1974–1978* (Paris: Unesco, 1982).
2. Elias Katsoulis, "Democrats against Colonels: Greeks in Germany from 1967 to 1974," in: *Landmarks of Greek-German relations*, ed. Evangelos Chrysos, Wolfgang Schultheiss (Athens: Foundation of the Greek Parliament for Parliamentarism and Democracy, 2010), 295.
3. *Between Marx and Coca-Cola: Youth Cultures in Changing European Societies 1960–1980*, ed. Axel Schildt, Detlef Siegfried (New York: Berghahn, 2006).
4. *Open letter*, Paris, Angelos Elefantis-Angelos Gogolos Collection, Archives of Contemporary Social History Athens [ASKI], April 1967.
5. Collection of resolutions of the Ordinary Assembly, Angelos Elefantis-Angelos Gogolos Collection, ASKI, 1972.
6. Report of the Board of Directors, internal text, Paris, Angelos Elefantis-Angelos Gogolos Collection, ASKI.
7. Nicos Hadjinicolaou, personal interview with the author, 17 April 2017.
8. The conference was attended by members of the Greek student associations of England, West and East Germany, France, Italy, Austria, Belgium, Switzerland, Hungary, Bulgaria, Czechoslovakia, Romania and the USSR. See the letters of the Greek unions and associations to the organizing committee with the legal documents of participation in Yianis Yanoulopoulos Collection, box 9, folder 58, Company for the Study of Left Youth History (EMIAN), May 1967.
9. Among the international student associations which greeted the conference were the National Student Unions of France (UNEF), USSR, Poland, Bulgaria, Czechoslovakia, Hungary, Tunisia, Morocco, Algeria, the Student Union of Puerto Rico, the Free Vietnam Students' Union, the North Vietnam National Student Union, the unions of Cuba, Bolivia, Kuwait, Iraq and the United Arab Republic. See "Chronicle: The pan-European conference," in: *Poreia*, vol. 2, June 1967, 36.
10. Ibid.
11. Makis Kavouriaris, personal interview with the author, 8 December 2016.
12. Pan-European Congress of Greek Students Abroad – Resolutions, Paris, Yianis Yanoulopoulos Collection, folder 58.4, EMIAN, May 1967.
13. Ibid.
14. Vangelis Karamanolakis, "The resistance of young people against the dictatorial regime," in: *The military dictatorship 1967–1974*, ed. Vangelis Karamanolakis (Athens: DOL, 2010), special edition for *Ta Nea*, 131–134.
15. The text of the report states that "in order to overthrow the dictatorship that was forcibly imposed in Greece, it is necessary to use every means, violent or not, to achieve this goal". See Pan-European Congress of Greek Students Abroad – Resolutions, ibid.
16. Gerasimos Notaras, "Dictatorship and organized resistance," in: *The dictatorship 1967–1974: political practices – ideological discourse – resistance*, ed. Gianna Athanasatou, Alkis Rigos, Serafeim Seferiadis (Athens: Kastaniotis, 1999), 191.
17. Report of the Board of Directors, ibid.
18. Ibid.
19. Ibid.
20. Anti-fascist Movement of Greece Abroad (A. K. E.), *Prospectus*, Archive of Anti-dictatorship Proclamations and Brochures, ASKI, [1968].
21. "Dynamic resistance and 21/4/67: the ghost of the armed struggle," in: *Ios tis Kyriakis* (insert in *Eleftherotypia*), April 2003, http://www.iospress.gr/ios2003/ios200304 20a.htm (last access 19 October 2022).
22. What came out of the European Conference, Angelos Elefantis-Angelos Gogolos Collection, ASKI, Paris, June 1967.
23. "Dynamic resistance and 21/4/67: The ghost of the armed struggle," ibid.

24 "Thoughts on the student movement abroad," in: *Poreia* vol. 12, October 1969, 9.
25 Angelos Elefantis, a postgraduate student, a leading member of the E.D.A. youth organization and a member of the student union in Paris, attempted to summarize the causes and impact of the Communist Party split at all political and social levels in an important text in anti-dictatorial magazine *Agonas*. See Angelos Elefantis, [A. Kranis], "Some views of Chaos or the chaos of some views," in:, *Agonas – Problems of modern politics*, vol. 2, February 1971, 27–40.
26 Ioanna Papathanassiou, "The Left: from the imposition of dictatorship to division," in: Karamanolakis, *The military dictatorship 1967–1974*, 155–160.
27 For all the above, see George Papadimitriou, "The ineffective effort of the dictatorial regime for the constitutional organization," in: Athanasatou, *The dictatorship 1967–1974*, 53–56; Konstantina Botsiou, "The Crown's relations with the dictatorship of the colonels," in: *The dictatorship of the colonels and the restoration of democracy (conference proceedings)*, ed. Pavlos Sourlas (Athens: Foundation of the Greek Parliament for Parliamentarism and Democracy, 2016), 113–136; Christos Christidis, "Europe versus the dictatorship of the colonels: the Greek case in the Council of Europe," in: Sourlas, *The dictatorship of the Colonels*, 405–420.
28 Gerasimos Notaras, "Dictatorship and organized resistance," in: Athanasatou, *The dictatorship 1967–1974*, 187–191.
29 2nd European Congress of Greek Students Abroad: Resolutions, Yianis Yanoulopoulos Collection, folder 57, EMIAN, London, July 1969.
30 For these considerations see indicatively: "The resistance and the Patriotic Anti-dictatorship Front," in: *Agonas: Problems of modern politics* 2, February 1971, 9–21; Nicos Hadjinicolaou [M. Paschalis], "Where is the resistance?," in: *Poreia*, vol. 9, November 1968, 16–27; AMEE, *Contribution to the development of the student movement: Education and the student movement of our country before and after the coup*, ASKI 12 (1970).
31 2nd European Congress of Greek Students Abroad – Resolutions, ibid.
32 Jürgen Habermas, "New Social Movements," in: *Telos* 49, October 1981, 33–37; Jürgen Habermas, *Toward A Rational Society: Student Protest, Science, and Politics*, (Boston: Beacon, 1989).
33 "Thoughts on the student movement abroad," in: *Poreia*, vol. 12, October 1969, 9.
34 Ibid.
35 The representatives came from clubs in England, West. Germany, France, Italy, Sweden, Norway, Denmark, Austria, Switzerland, the Netherlands, the USSR, Hungary, Romania, Bulgaria. See "The third conference of the EFEE abroad," in: *Eleftheri Ellada*, Period B, no. 13 (164), February 1971, 1.
36 "The student movement: The Third Pan-European Congress (Copenhagen 20–22 Jan. 1971)," in: *Poreia*, vol. 17, February 1971, 9.
37 "The student movement," in: *Poreia*, vol. 16, October 1970, 55–56.
38 About the concerns of the administrations of many Greek student associations throughout Europe, see "The Greek student movement: contributions to the preparation of the Third Pan-European Conference," in: *Poreia*, vol. 15, July 1970, 30–31; "The student movement," in: *Poreia*, vol. 16, ibid., 60–61.
39 "Thoughts on the student movement abroad," ibid., 8.
40 Collection of resolutions of the Ordinary Assembly, ibid.
41 The members who left on the last day of the conference were representatives of the Greek student associations of the USSR (based in Tashkent), Hungary, Bulgaria and two of the four delegates of the Bologna union. See "The third conference of the EFEE abroad," in: *Eleftheri Ellada*, ibid.
42 Dimitris Vlantos joined the local youth organization of the Greek Communist Party in the period 1971–1972, while at the same time he had a significant presence in the ac-

tivities and mobilizations of the communist party in West Germany. See Dimitris Vlantos, personal interview with the author, February 2021.
43 "The student movement: Third Pan-European Congress (Copenhagen 20–22 Jan. 1971)," in: *Poreia,* ibid., 10–11.
44 Ibid., 9–11.
45 "The third conference of the EFEE abroad," in: *Eleftheri Ellada,* ibid., 1, 4.
46 "The Stockholm Student Association Condemns the Splitters," in: *Eleftheri Patrida,* Second Period, no. 16 (167), February 1971, 3.
47 "The student movement: The Third European Congress (Copenhagen 20–22 Jan. 1971)," ibid., 10; "An action," in: *Start,* vol. 1 [November 1971], 34; AMEE, The Third Conference of Greek antifascists Student Associations abroad, Angelos Elephantis Collection, ASKI, February 1971.
48 "SEFL and its perspectives" in: *Foititiki Protoporia,* vol. 1, October 1972, 4.
49 "On the literature around the student movement abroad," in:, *Poreia,* vol. 19, February 1972, 47–53.
50 AMEE, The Third Conference of the Greek Antifascist Student Associations abroad, ibid.
51 AASPE, Action Plan of AASPE West. Berlin, Anna Filini Archive, ASKI, West Berlin, 1972.
52 Charles Tilly, *Social Movements 1768–2004,* (London: Paradigm, 2004), 65–71.
53 Martin Klimke, Joachim Scharloth, "1968 in Europe: An Introduction," in: *1968 in Europe,* ed. id., 5.

Dimitrios Garris

Alekos Panagoulis: The Genesis of an Anti-Dictatorship Hero (1968–1976)

In September 2019, Attiko Metro, the company operating the Athens Metro-railway, announced the renaming of two stations. *Evangelismos* would be replaced by *Pavlos Bakoyannis* and *Agios Dimitrios* (St. Dimitrios) would be renamed as *Alexandros Panagoulis*. According to the company's announcement, "the main goal of Attiko Metro renaming the two stations is to serve as a constant reminder of the values of democracy, freedom and national reconciliation"[1]. Both Pavlos Bakoyannis and Alexandros Panagoulis are prominent figures of the anti-dictatorship resistance, Bakoyannis notable for his opposition through the microphones of the Bayerischer Rundfunk (the Bavarian public broadcasting station in Germany), and Panagoulis for his dynamic anti-dictatorship action in Greece.

Of the two, the focus of this paper is on the latter. Alexandros Panagoulis is today considered a hero with high visibility in Greece. An imposing statue of him in Panepistimiou Street, one of the most central streets of Athens, his name now alongside that of St. Dimitrios in the metro station, numerous smaller roads and public squares bearing his name, together with several songs of Mikis Theodorakis attest to his well-established Panagoulis' heroic status.

The subject of this paper is the construction of an anti-dictatorship hero, in the case of Alekos Panagoulis. The resistance against the military dictatorship supplied the collective imagination of the Third Greek Republic[2] with heroic actors, collective and individual. If on the level of collective hero, *Athens Polytechnic University* ('Polytechnio') and its uprising in November 1973 have the unrivalled dominance, the following hypothesis focuses on the fact that Panagoulis takes the first place among the individual heroes of the Greeks' struggle against the dictatorship. The author's goal is to take Panagoulis as an illustrative example of one individual hero who became a symbol of the entire anti-dictatorship resistance movement in the collective narrative of the Greek public. The paper traces the conditions and mechanisms through which this heroic figure was formed and attempts to shed light on the practices contributing to the construction of the symbol 'Panagoulis', the elements of the hero identity which was attributed to him, as well as who were the constituents of the *memory communities* involved in the making of this hero. One of the central concerns of this contribution is to study the construction of a modern hero and, concurrently, how the culture of remembrance plays a crucial role in the iconic status Panagoulis holds today.

Before we proceed to the main part of the paper, two remarks are necessary. Firstly, due to the restricted extent of the following text, the main emphasis is placed in the hero-making discourse during the junta and until Panagoulis' death in 1976. Secondly, due to the very nature of the topic under investigation, the discussion of German involvement is limited.

Alekos Panagoulis' Anti-Dictatorship Works & Days

Alexandros Panagoulis was born in Glyfada, a suburb south of Athens, in 1939. His first entry to politics was through the youth organisation of the Centre Union party, known as ONEK, and fighting for democratic values during the turbulent 'Greek Sixties'. The coup of April 1967 found him serving his military service in Veria, a small town of northern Greece. A few days later, Panagoulis deserted the Greek army in order to organise his anti-dictatorship activities. He founded the organisation Greek Resistance (*Elliniki Antistasi*) and on 13 August 1968, with the help of his numbered comrades, he ventured an assassination attempt against the leader of junta, Georgios Papadopoulos, close to Lagonisi, the seaside residential area where the dictator's villa was located. The attempt failed and Panagoulis was arrested the same day. In November 1968, he was put on trial in military court, bearing evident marks of having been tortured, and was sentenced to death on 17 November. Subsequently, he was transported to the island of Aegina for the sentence to be carried out. However, as a result of political pressure from the international community, the junta refrained from executing him and instead incarcerated him at Bogiati Military Prison, near Athens. Panagoulis refused to cooperate with the junta, and was subjected to ferocious physical and psychological torture during his detention. He escaped from prison on 5 June 1969. However, he was soon arrested again and placed in solitary confinement at Bogiati, from which he then attempted to escape unsuccessfully on several occasions. In August 1973, after five years in jail, he benefited from a general amnesty that the military regime granted to all political prisoners during a failed attempt by Papadopoulos to liberalise his regime. When junta hardliners seized power, Panagoulis chose to go into exile in Florence, Italy, in order to continue the resistance. There, he stayed with Oriana Fallaci, his companion, who then became his biographer.[3]

Less than a year later, the junta collapsed and democracy was restored in a period called *Metapolitefsi* ('regime change'). Panagoulis was elected as Member of Parliament for the party Centre Union – New Forces (*Enosis Kentrou – Nees Dynameis*) in the November 1974 elections. As an MP, he took on dynamic action to rid the state machinery of those who had collaborated with the junta. Major moments in his battle for 'catharsis'(purification) were the acquisition of the Greek military police archives of the junta period, known as 'ESA archives', and the subsequent publication of some of these documents in an influential Greek newspaper in late April 1976. Four days after its beginning, the publication of the archives was stopped by a restraining order issued by the military court. One week later, on 1st May 1976, Panagoulis was killed in a controversial car accident on Vouliagmenis Avenue in Athens. For Monday, 3 May 1976, he had announced the revelation of the sealed archives in the Parliament.[4]

Memorializing Panagoulis: A provocateur, a legend or a martyr?

The following sections demonstrate how, over the next decades of the Third Greek Republic following the *Metapolitefsi* of 1974, Panagoulis progressively became a widely accepted hero and the unifying symbol of a past era of both authoritarian repression and heroic resistance.

Returning to the very first period of the hero-making process, during the dictatorship and until Panagoulis' death, we can ascertain that his heroic status was not yet a given and the categorisation of Panagoulis as a symbol of the entire resistance movement came as a result of various and complicated processes, full of contingencies and without any kind of teleology. During that first period, when Panagoulis was still alive, we observe the existence of a 'pendulum' whose oscillation certifies that Panagoulis had not yet been entered permanently into a heroic pantheon. Therefore, in the time span between the heroic act – the attempt on the dictator's life – and the hero's death, we detect a non-linear, ambivalent process during which the heroic identity of Panagoulis was still under negotiation and certainly unstable.

Panagoulis' death in May 1976 can be identified as a turning point at which the 'pendulum' receives a major push, and afterwards swings greatly to the side of the heroic. The cause of the car crash which killed him remains controversial to this day. Death marked a crucial, radically transformative point in the hero-making procedure. Thenceforth, the dynamics of *heroisation* would be reoriented in a more systematic and intensive way. As Oriana Fallaci writes in her Panagoulis' biography: "There is no living hero worth as much as a dead hero."[5]

During the dictatorship, there were mainly two mechanisms

through which the *symbol* 'Panagoulis' began to be constructed. The first were the press releases of anti-dictatorship organisations and the second was a relatively small number of texts, such as books that attempted a first *narrativisation* of the Panagoulis' case. It is noteworthy that, until the fall of Colonels' regime, the biggest part of the *heroisation* took part abroad, in Western Europe and in North America, where active communities of Greek immigrants and students existed. This included various West German cities, especially Munich with the notable example of Pavlos Bakoyannis' radio broadcasts against the Greek military junta on the radio station *Bayerischer Rundfunk*.[6] In November 1968, after the suspension of Panagoulis' death penalty, Bakoyannis pointed out on the air:

> "The suspension of the execution of the sentence imposed on Alexandros Panagoulis relieved the souls of thousands of people. Panagoulis with his case gave the opportunity to reveal the global lack of trust in the Colonels.[...] Panagoulis humiliated the regime and the regime was forced to accept the humiliation."[7]

However, due to pre-existing bonds of Panagoulis' organisation with Italy, it is that country which played the central role in supporting the resistance movement.

Inside these two corpora of sources (produced during the dictatorship), one can observe the aforementioned ambivalence about Panagoulis and his assassination attempt. One might assume that references related to Panagoulis were divided into heroic on the one hand and heretic on the other. A fruitful way to understand these counterbalancing forces that coexist during the first phase of the *herois*ation process may be to think of it as moving between two pairs.

At the first pair, the act and the person, namely the assassination attempt against the dictator and Alekos Panagoulis, coexist and are juxtaposed. In a large share of the anti-dictatorship press, mainly newspapers of leftist organisations, a certain reluctance or suspicion towards Panagoulis and his assassination attempt are evident. Two days after the attempt, the Greek Communist party, KKE, as expressed through its radio station 'Voice of Truth', rejected individual 'dynamic action' (a term commonly used by anti-dictatorship actors to denote armed resistance) as means of anti-dictatorship resistance and implied that Panagoulis may have been a provocateur hired or encouraged by the junta.[8] Similarly, the anti-dictatorship newspaper *Resistance*, published by a Trotskyist group in Paris, not merely criticised the attempt but condemned it sharply while also calling its authenticity into question.[9]

The dualism between a 'rejectable attempted murder' and a 'praiseworthy personality' of Panagoulis was imprinted, in a more concrete way, in Yannis Katris' book *Eyewitness in Greece: The Rise of Neofascism*, which was published in 1971[10]. In this book, the attempt was judged as "the impulsive outburst of a group of anti-fascist citizens" and was assessed as "politically unsuitable action". Katris pointed out that "the failed attempt did not benefit the struggle of the Greek people, just as no nihilistic act ever benefited the popular movements". But when it comes to Panagoulis, the author had a completely different attitude as far as he was treated like an indisputable hero. The most interesting element is that, in Katris' book Panagoulis was not the possible provocateur of the first months but he had not yet become the "glorious tyrannicide", insofar as his heroic charge was originated from his courageous stance in the trial, from his superhuman endurance of torture and not from the attempt against Papadopoulos.[11]

1972 was to be a crucial year in the *heroisation* process of Panagoulis involving two critical developments, which both have had a strong effect on the way that Panagoulis' legend was constructed from then on. Firstly, in 1972 two books were published which tried to capture Panagoulis' story in its entirety: *Portrait of a fighter: Nikos Zampelis* of Vassilis Vassilikos was published around the end of 1972 in Rome and the Amalia Fleming's *A Piece of Truth* at the same period in Boston,

USA (1973). An important detail is that both books were 'insider' versions: Zambelis, who was the narrator-informant in the work of Vassilikos, was one of Panagoulis' closest companions in the preparation and execution of the attempt, while Fleming also had a crucial organisational role in a failed attempt to help Panagoulis escape from military prison in August 1971.

The second significant development, which came in 1972, has to do with the legitimising construction through which the attempt could be registered into heroic genealogies that would render Panagoulis' act acceptable and praiseworthy. Fleming in her book parallels Panagoulis with the tyrannicides Harmodius and Aristogeiton of classical Athens. In this re-telling, Panagoulis became the tyrannicide who puts his life at risk in order to defend democracy. The attempt henceforward could be positively presented inasmuch as "Tyrants' killing is a duty and glory be owed to tyrannicides."[12]

Passing to the second pair, here the 'pendulum' oscillates between victimization and heroization. Here, of central importance are the torture that Panagoulis suffered during his detention. More specifically, after the prevention of his execution in November 1968, in the pages of antidictatorship Press was about to begin a long-rebroadcast procedure of Panagoulis' pain. Until August 1973 and his liberation, numerous articles were published with titles like: "Panagoulis: His life in danger" or "Save Panagoulis!". In these appeals Panagoulis was projected as the junta's biggest victim. We read in the bulletin of Union of Democratic Youth of Munich, in the August 1972 issue: "The dictators didn't kill Panagoulis in order to see him dying alive in jail. (…) We must not allow his martyrdom remains a simple pain, we have to act"[13]. In the same vein, in a Nikos Zampelis' article of April 1973, in the antidictatorship newspaper *Struggle* (Agonas), Panagoulis was projected as the martyr who was extremely close to sacrifice. We read: "How long will this man endure his constant torment? He lives? Or he is fighting with death?"[14]. In June 1972, thirty-three political prisoners of Korydallos' prisons, in the appeal they wrote "for the salvation of Al. Panagoulis" they were wondering: "How long can one survive without facing the sun?".[15] Furthermore, it is noteworthy that, except the Greek antidictatorship Press, we can detect similar appeals and in the German newspapers. For example, in the *Westf. Volksblatt,* which was published in Paderborn, we read: "The Greek man sentenced to death Alexandros Panagoulis appealed to all free people for support. (…) Panagoulis begs to get out of his dirty cell even for a while and face the sun or to speed up his execution".[16]

However, in Panagoulis' case, his martyrdom did not bring about a dominance of the victim identity in the long run. An instance of the fluctuation between the hero and victim attributions can be found in the coexistence of two classic heroic archetypes in the foreword proposed by Fallaci in Panagoulis' first interview after his release in August 1973, as published a month later in the Italian magazine *L'Europeo*. The two heroic archetypes were Christ and Odysseus.[17] Panagoulis may have endured the scars of torture "to the place where the wounds of Christ were", but his rebellious spirit and his great ingenuity in the ways of enduring martyrdom more closely resembled the Homeric hero. In other words, next to the image of the tortured martyr there was, and in the course of time was becoming stronger, the image of the untamed and most courageous fighter; the image of whom has had suffered hell on earth but he had been the only one that did not break. The very idea that crops up in a verse of Panagoulis' own poetry, oftentimes reproduced in the anti-dictatorship press: "I want to win since I cannot be defeated"[18].

Writing the story of Alexandros Panagoulis

The first two years of *Metapolitefsi*, from the junta's fall and until the moment of Panagoulis' death (1974–1976), mark the only period after the assassination attempt during which Panagoulis was alive, free and in Greece at the same time. The author Vassilis Vasilikos, who as early as in 1972 had written a first account of the attack in his book *Portrait of a fighter: Nikos Zampelis*[19], urged Panagoulis to write "the true story of the attempt" himself after 1974.[20] It seems that Panagoulis did not dislike this idea as, in the spring of 1976 he started writing a book to tell his story.[21] He managed to write only twenty-three pages in which the narrative begins on 13 August 1968 (the day of the attempted assassination) and ends with a description of the torturing he suffered after his arrest in the EAT-ESA camp (Military Police 'Special Interrogation' Unit).

These manuscripts are undeniably important, but not because of the information they reveal. Besides, only a few days are narrated there. Apart from the general historical value that the manuscripts of any pioneer fighter of the anti-dictatorship struggle have, which element gives a special interest to Panagoulis' pages in the context of the hero-making? Simply: the fact that Panagoulis wanted to write a book. Narrating his side of the story would have given him the opportunity to create his own public image. That in itself is something assessable. While being alive, Panagoulis realised the heroism attributed to him, and he wanted to have a say in the composition of Panagoulis the hero. In August 1973, a few days after his release, he told Fallaci: "I am neither a hero nor do I feel like a hero. I am not a symbol, nor do I see myself as a hero. (…) I'm so scared I might disappoint you! If you could only see me not as a hero!"[22]

This passage is insightful as it reveals that Panagoulis, already in 1973, realised that he had been *heroised*. In the circles of anti-dictatorship resistance, he was considered a hero, despite his contrary assurances.

A moving on once more to the period of 1974–76, we can find out if and how Panagoulis contributed to the construction of his heroic profile towards the end of his life. The fall of the dictatorship and the restoration of democracy in the summer of 1974 radically changed the dynamics of collective memory. During the first years of the after the regime change, the living memory of the heroes of the anti-dictatorship struggle experienced moments of quantitative explosion as the newly formed democracy had an organic need to give prominence to the heroic figures of the anti-dictatorship resistance. In this way, the Third Greek Republic established a strong heroic narrative at its birth, which inspired confidence within the collective imagination and at the same time had a soothing effect, contributing to the gradual weakening of the feeling of unacknowledged guilt which had set in regarding the passive tolerance that the majority of Greek society had shown towards the junta.

In the second half of 1974, we can distinguish two actions of Panagoulis which contributed to or directed his *heroisation*. First, his return to Athens from Rome, after the fall of the junta. The anti-dictatorship fighter chose to return to Greece on 13 August 13, 1974, the sixth anniversary of the assassination attempt because, as he had confessed to Fallaci, "the idea of refreshing the memory of some amuses me a lot".[23] In addition to the symbolic choice of date, Panagoulis had also ensured that the news of his return was channelled to the Greek press. However, besides these elements of self-direction, there elements of external heroisation are also evident. The slogans written on the placards at Elliniko Airport in Athens on the afternoon of Panagoulis' return broadcasts epitomise the tone. The most symbolic message reads: "Politechnio [Athens Polytechnic uprising of November 1973] salutes the tyrannicide", when in another we read: "Do not cry for the brave man, even if he missed the target"[24].[25] Thus, in a festive and vindictive atmosphere, some of the people gathered there, eventually wore a laurel wreath to Panagoulis and then lifted him in their arms.[26]

Looking back at Panagoulis' election posters,[27] we have the opportunity to make a safer assessment of the way he personally used his symbolic anti-dictatorship capital in a political context. One campaign poster showed two photos, each accompanied by a date and a message. In the first one, Panagoulis was depicted during his trial in the military court, and the caption he chose reads: "November 17, 1968: The junta sentenced him to death twice." In the second photo, Panagoulis posed for the camera with a jacket and tie in a typical photo of a parliamentary candidate; the caption urged: "November 17, 1974: The people will condemn fascism with their vote." Voters were called on to elect him in order to prove "that the people do not forget the one who wanted to free them from tyranny."

Another of Panagoulis election campaign leaflets lists what he would offer as a deputy in the parliament. Two elements are interesting here. The first is the fact that half of the pamphlet was covered by excerpts from Panagoulis' *apologia* (defence statement) in the junta's military court. He quoted, for example, his famous concluding phrase: "the most beautiful swan song of any real fighter is the death rattle in front of the firing squad of tyranny." It thus becomes clear that the *apologia* evolved into (and was stylised by him as) his most important verbal legacy from the dictatorship period, and that he used it as a credential, hoping it would allow him to enter the first freely elected parliament after 1974. The second noteworthy element of the pamphlet is the promise of the last line: "His presence in Parliament is a guarantee that the crimes of the junta will not go unpunished." This commitment to the punishment of the junta's pioneers introduces us to a new semantic field of heroisation, namely that of *dynamic catharsis*, which was to dominate in the heroic process in the last year-and-a-half of Panagoulis' life, culminating in the unfinished revelation of the ESA archives.

Conclusion

Panagoulis was once perceived as a liability within the resistance movement and was later re-branded as an epic fighter for the cause. His untimely death contributed to the *heroisation* of is person by signalling two developments. Firstly, although Panagoulis was an independent agent for the last three months before his death, immediately after his demise he was claimed as a symbol – as he remains today, by all political parties, except the far right. With his death, the once contradictory and inconvenient aspects of the living Panagoulis transformed into a unifying quality for the symbol that Panagoulis became. Arguably, there was no one else more suitable than him to become the first hero of the newly restored democracy. Secondly, the near universal feeling in May 1976 that Panagoulis had been assassinated was related with another component of Panagoulis' heroic identity. Louis Danos, a journalist in the Greek newspaper *Elefthero-typia* ('Free Press'), presented Panagoulis as the person who had "revealed the Greek Watergate".[28],[29] A plaque on Panagoulis' coffin reads: "In 1968 Alexandros Panagoulis was condemned to death because he searched for freedom. In 1976 Alexandros died because he searched for truth and he found it".[30] The second sentence of the above phrase alludes to two obscurities on which, even today, we cannot rule categorically. Nor can one claim with certainty that Panagoulis had indeed found the truth about what he was looking for – Cyprus and the *coup d'*état by Ioannidis; the disappearance of his brother, George Panagoulis; relations between government agents and junta agents during the dictatorship – nor that even if he had actually found the truth, he was killed because of it, as to date it has not been proven that his death was a murder. However, these two phrases written on the coffin of Panagoulis are important insofar as they convey the atmosphere of the time.

His last act – the struggle for the release of the ESA archive – was in absolute accordance with the prevailing mood at a moment when, two years after the junta's fall, the majority of Greek public opinion admitted that complete catharsis had not been achieved. They demanded disassociation from and punishment of the junta, and the consolidation of democracy. Thus, rather than representing a discrete ideology, Panagoulis became a common denominator of anti-dictatorship resistance and of passionate democratic commitment, a symbol with multiple possibilities.

Another interesting element is that Panagoulis in the period 1974–76 actively intervened in the formation of his legend. At first glance, his manner might seem clumsy or out of place, however, it would be misleading to see his intervention as something rare or reprehensible. Panagoulis is not exceptional in this context but rather within the norm. In the first years after the fall of the junta, there was an explosion of testimonies about the anti-dictatorship struggle. Protagonists and ordinary participants of the resistance wrote, published, and issued testimonies. In other words, at that very moment, a democratisation of memory took place, Panagoulis, the almost tyrannicide.

1   "The metro stations 'Evangelismos' and 'Agios Dimitrios' would be renamed", Efimerida ton Syntakton [Editors' Journal] 20 September 2019, https://www.efsyn.gr/node/211587 (last access 8 October 2021).
2   The *Third Greek Republic* is the period in modern Greek history that stretches from 1974, with the fall of the military junta and the final abolition of the monarchy, to the present day.
3   Oriana Fallaci, *Enas Andras [A Man]* (Athens: Exantas, 1980).
4   For more information about Panagoulis' life see: Tasos Sakellaropoulos, "Resistance 1967–1974: Political pressure, dynamic actions," in: Vasilis Panayiotopoulos (ed.), *History of New Hellenism 1770–2000, vol. 9* (Athens: Ellinika Grammata, 2003), 135–142; Achileas Hatzopoulos, *Oi deka meres tou Mai [The ten days of May]* (Athens: Papazisis, 1976), 9–14.
5   Fallaci, *Enas Andras*, 449 and 481.
6   For Bakoyannis' antidictatorship action, see Nikos Papanastasiou, *Resistance via microphone: Pavlos Bakoyannis against the Colonels' Dictatorship* (Athens: Papadopoulos, 2020).
7   Pavlos Bakoyannis, "A dictatorship is humiliated," *Pressespiegel der IG Metall für die Griechischen Kollegen* 53 (December 1968), 3.
8   "And the Communist Party (KKE) disapproves," *Akropolis* 12577 (17.08.1968), 1.
9   "Announcement," *Resistance* no. 9 (July–August 1968), 8.
10 Simultaneously a Greek edition in Western Europe and an English one in the US and Canada (Yannis Katris, *Ellada 1960–1970 – I Gennisi tou Neofasismou*, Washington, Geneve: Editex, 1971).
11 Yannis Katris, *Eyewitness in Greece: The Rise of Neofascism* (Athens: Papazisis, 1974), 330.
12 Amalia Fleming, *A Piece of Truth* (Athens: Estia, 1995), 99–101.
13 G. Politis, "Stamatiste ta vasanistiria [Stop the tortures]," in: *Deltio Enimeroseos – Miniaio organo tis EK-EDIN Monahou [Bulletin of information. Monthly instrument of Union of Democratic Youth of Munich]* no. 13, August 1972, 9.
14 Nikos Zampelis, "I zoi tou Al. Panagouli se kindino [Panagoulis' life in danger]," in: *Agonas – Dekapenthimero eleuthero elliniko dimosiografiko organo [Struggle. Free Greek Journalistic Instrument]* no. 74, 28 April 1973, 2.
15 "Gia ti sotiria tou Alekou Panagouli [For the salvation of Al. Panagoulis]", *Agonas – Dekapenthimero eleuthero elliniko dimosiografiko organo [Struggle. Free Greek Journalistic Instrument]* no. 68, 2 September 1972, 2.
16 "Panagoulis asks for some sun," *Westf. Volksblatt*, 10 March 1969.
17 Oriana Fallaci, *Synantisi me tin Istoria [Interview with History]* (Athens: Papyrus, 1976), 550, 553, 555, 560–561.
18 Alexandros Panagoulis, *Ta poiimata [The poems]* (Athens: Papazisis, 2010), 88.
19 Vassilis Vassilikos, *Portreto enos agonisti:*

  Nikos Zampelis [*Portrait of a fighter: Nikos Zampelis*] (Rome: 8 ½, 1973).
20 Vassilis Vassilikos, *Sarx and Marx, Travelogues, Monologues, The shock of nature, Panagoulis lives* (Athens: G. Ladia, 1977), 498–499.
21 Fallaci, *Enas Andras,* 40 and 409–423.
22 Fallaci, *Synantisi me tin istoria,* 605–606.
23 Fallaci, *Enas Andras,* 280.
24 "Τον αντρειωμένο μην τον κλαις, μηδέ κι αν αστοχήσει".
25 Kostas Mardas, *Alexandros Panagoulis. Death rehearsals* (Athens: private edition, 1997), 388–390; George Athanasiades, Markos Marinakis, Kostas Tsipiras, *In Alekos Panagoulis' memory* (Athens: Kastaniotis, 1977), 74.
26 Nana Ntaoudaki, "A laurel wreath for Panagoulis," in: *Athinaiki* 19, 14 August 1974, 3.
27 For the posters and leaflets commented here, see Athanasiades, *In Alekos Panagoulis' memory,* 84–85.
28 Louis Danos, "Panagoulis revealed the Greek Watergate," in: *Eleftherotypia* 242, 8 May 1976, 4.
29 This was a direct reference to Panagoulis' incomplete attempt to open the military police archives of the junta period to the public. According to Panagoulis, the disclosure of these archives would contribute decisively to a 'catharsis' of state machinery, removing them from the control of those which had collaborated with the Colonels.
30 Hatzopoulos, *Oi deka meres tou Mai,* 110.

Loukas Bartatilas

Solidarity Networks in Architecture: Akademie der Künste and Ioannis Despotopoulos

This paper focuses on a less known aspect of Greek-German relations: architecture. It is mainly based on the archival material which exists in the Archives of the Akademie der Künste (AdK)[1] in Berlin, and is presented to the public for the first time. Its theme is the support provided by the architects and members of the AdK during the Greek military dictatorship to their colleague, architect Ioannis Despotopoulos. Although it is a small-scale example, as it refers to the actions of the members of a cultural organisation towards a specific person, it should be considered as one case in a series of activities, which reflect the solidarity between the two countries during that time.[2]

The Akademie der Künste

The Akademie der Künste (AdK) was founded in 1696 and is one of the oldest cultural institutions in Europe.[3] Today, the AdK has an extensive archive considered to be one of the most important interdisciplinary archives for the arts of the 20th century. The importance of the AdK in the cultural landscape of Germany can also be seen in the location of its two buildings. The main building is located at Pariser Platz[4], right next to the Brandenburg Gate, the most central and historically meaningful part of the city. The other building is in *Hansaviertel*, the most representative neighborhood of West Berlin architecture,[5] during the Cold War.

In 1783, Daniel Chodowiecki, an early member of AdK's historic predecessor organisation *Königlich-Preußische Akademie der Künste und mechanischen Wissenschaften* (Royal Prussian Akademy of the Arts and Mechanical Sciences), formulated a definition of an *academy*: he stated that an academy is, among other things, an assembly of artists who meet regularly, communicate in a friendly manner, share observations and experiences, and learn from each other.[6] Today, this definition is projected on a video wall at the main building entrance, showing the impact Chodowiecki's words have on work of the AdK until this day.

In addition to the previous definition, AdK members drafted a policy statement in 1966 describing the goals of the academy as a cultural institution. The statement said that the goal of the AdK is, among other things, to oppose anything that threatens the arts and moreover to protect open discussion in the world, since art is a common language for all people.[7] Chodowiecki's definition and the 1966 policy statement describe the philosophy of the AdK and the spirit of cooperation and mutual support between its members, which we will see in the case of Ioannis Despotopoulos.

Ioannis Despotopoulos a. k. a. Jan Despo

Ioannis Despotopoulos was known in Germany as Jan Despo. He was the only Greek architect who came in direct contact with the Bauhaus school, when he lived in Weimar between 1922–1923.[8] His experience of the cultural environment of the Weimar Republic and the socialist ideas of modernism and urban planning in Germany of that time, strongly influenced him and shaped his theoretical work.

During the Nazi occupation of Greece, Despo became a professor at the School of Architecture of the National Technical University of Athens (NTUA). Moreover, in the first years after Greece's liberation, he became one of the leading members of EPAN,[9] a group that developed an elaborate academic and theoretical framework[10] for the reconstruction of the country after the damage to society and infrastructure suffered during World War II. Several articles by Despo on the topic were published in *Antaios* magazine. As a consequence of these activities and the ongoing Greek Civil War, Despo was fired from his university position in October 1946. With the support of his Bauhaus contacts, he escaped[11] to Sweden in early 1947 in order to avoid to be send in exile as many of his colleagues. In Sweden Despo remained for 14 years. There, he participated in many architectural conferences, meeting the most important German architects of the time. He developed long and fruitful contacts with them, which would be reflected in his election as a temporary member of the AdK in 1964.[12]

Despo returned to Athens in 1961, meanwhile having won first prize in the 1959 architectural competition for the design of the Cultural Centre of Athens (CCA). For this proposal, Despo faced a great wave of criticism from the majority of his Greek colleagues which almost amounted to personal bullying.[13] A few years later, the military regime decided to build a war museum inside the field where the Cultural Centre was supposed to be built, ignoring Despo's award-winning proposal. This made the realisation of this significant project for the city of Athens impossible. As a result, Despo became a virtual recluse, with trips to Berlin for AdK meetings as his only fruitful and honest social gatherings.

The meeting of the Academy in Athens

During the regular assembly in Berlin in 1965, the Academy members discussed the possibility of holding the next meeting in a foreign city for the first time. They chose Athens, the city where the first Academy was created some thousand years ago[14] – a symbolic choice which gave AdK members the message of a democratic direction.[15] The meeting[16] took place from April 3–10, 1967, just two weeks before the military coup. Martin Heidegger, himself a member of the AdK, came to Athens and gave a lecture at the Academy of Athens, which Panayiotis Kannelopoulos, Greece's Prime Minister at that time, attended. Despo's involvement in the preparation of that trip and his idea to bring both academies into contact, was very much appreciated by his German colleagues.

Despo's election as a permanent member of the AdK (1967)

Just two days after the coup in Greece, the regular assembly of the AdK members convened in Berlin. The first item on the agenda was the promotion of Despo from temporary member of the AdK to permanent membership.[17] Despo was not able to attend the assembly[18], as his trip to Berlin was canceled at last minute due to the political developments in Greece.

For a long time, Despo did not contact the AdK, which had in the meantime notified him of his promotion. Having heard about Greece's situation, his colleagues in Germany were worried about his silence. The secretary of the Department of Architecture of the AdK, Peter Pfankuch, expressed his concern to the others through a note, wondering if Despo's silence was related to the current political situation.[19] Despo communicated with the AdK through a simple telegram for the first time on July 24, 1967, three months after the coup.[20] On the same day, he wrote a much more detailed letter to his friend, fellow academy member and former Bauhaus student Wilhelm Wagenfend.

From this letter[21], we learn that the AdK's meeting in Athens and the imposition of the dictatorship a few days later led him to experience intense contradictory feelings, creating the need for complete seclusion for some period of time to recover. The bad memories of the period following Greece's liberation in 1944, his forced escape to Sweden to avoid exile in 1947, his renewed fear of exile[22], and the possibility of complete cancellation of the CCA project were enough to petrify him.

This letter is also indicative of the feelings of appreciation Despo had for the AdK. Despo wrote to Wagenfeld that the experience he had visiting the archaeological site of Delphi with his Academy colleagues during the Athens meeting was a unique moment for him. He points out that the environment of the *academy* functions for him not only as an essential cultural forum, but also even more, as a place of spiritual and mental renewal.[23]

Dismissal from the NTUA (1968)

In October 1967, an article was published in the West-German press[24] stating that the Regime of the Colonels had suspended eleven university professors. The article even mentioned two of them by name, one of whom was Despo, a fact that illustrates the reputation and respect Despo enjoyed inside German academic and intellectual circles. As soon as they read the article, the members of the AdK discussed it and took immediate action.

One of its members, Hugo Hartung, sent a letter to the president of the AdK, Hans Scharoun, on the same day, asking him directly how the AdK could support their – as he phrased it – "likable colleague" under the Greek dictatorship.[25]

Two other members, Peter Löffler and Swiss architect Werner Moser corresponded about the same topic[26], Moser being old friend of Despo. Löffler expressed his concerns about the situation while highlighting the reputation Despo had abroad. Therefore, Löffler asked Moser if he thought that would be possible to extend an invitation from a Swiss university to Despo as a supportive gesture.

Help eventually came from Technische Universität (TU) Stuttgart, through Despo's AdK colleagues, Walter Rossow and Wilhelm Wagenfeld. They invited Despo to visit the University in the winter semester of 1968 for a series of lectures.[27] These direct responses from members, using the AdK network in order to offer solidarity and help a colleague, fully live up to the principles of Chodowiecki and the 1966 policy statement, proving in practice the higher purpose of the AdK.

Despo's 1973 book publication

During Berlin Architecture Week in September 1966, Despo gave a lecture titled "The ideological formation of cities"[28] which the AdK later decided to publish.[29] Despite this decision, the process proceeded slowly and six years later seemed to have come to a halt. In 1972, in a letter to his friend, architect and AdK member Bernhard Hermkes, Despo mentioned his surprise at the delay.[30] Hermkes took action and, in a letter to AdK secretary Hermann Fehling, emphasized[31] the importance of Despo's work in the context of the AdK, recalling the generous invitation of the Greek Government for the AdK meeting in Athens and the effort Despo put into preparing that trip.

Thus, after the intervention of Hermkes, the book was published in early 1973.[32] This book[33] would be something of great symbolic meaning and value for Despo. Since the cancellation of the CCA project and therefore his inability to leave a complete built work, this book would become his theoretical legacy. At the same time, this book stands as an example of Greek-German cooperation and exchange of knowledge in the field of architecture until today.

Correspondence between Despo and Hermkes during the dictatorship

The close and continuous communication between Jan Despo and Bernhard Hermkes started in 1965 on the occasion of the design of the Botanical Gardens of Athens by Hermkes with the assistance of Despo. Over the years, the two of them opened up more and more and from a certain point on they changed the way they addressed each other, adding the word "friend" in their salutations[34] – an essential step in developing a friendship the context of the German culture of personal contacts.

In December 1973, Hermkes wrote to Despo[35] shortly after the Polytechnic student uprising against the dictatorship in Greece. In Despo's response in May 1974, after a long hiatus, he appeared disappointed with political developments after November 1973 and hoped to come to Berlin for the Academy meeting to see Hermkes and his other friends for which he expressed a great need.[36]

In the next letter, shortly before the end of the dictatorship, Hermkes responded[37] emphasising that if he could support Despo in any way, he was ready to do so at any time.

Epilogue

Shortly after the re-establishment of democracy, Despo wrote a letter to Hermkes, which may be read today as a short chronicle of the early post-dictatorship era in Greece:

"Dear friend Hermkes,

> You know everything that has happened in Greece through the press. As in October 1944, the Greek people showed an admirable attitude and political maturity today, but not the politicians and their press.
>
> Let us hope that Karamanlis, who 'learned' a lot in Paris,[38] will receive a substantial majority in the elections [November 17th, 1974].
>
> Even the communists – the K. P. G. [Communist Party of Greece] was recently legitimised[39] – want such a majority for Karamanlis.
>
> 'Cyprus' is the issue that it is of great importance for the development and existence of Greece.[40] The evolution will show it. The press reported that Karamanlis had decided in favor of the rapid implementation of the Cultural Center [CCA]; it was his own idea after all.
>
> We are in Vouliagmeni, where I seek rest and relaxation. The weather, the calm landscape with the clear colors and the gentle sun are really a magic of beauty."[41]

It is important to note the parallel Despo drew between the liberation of Greece from the Nazis in October 1944 and the establishment of democracy in July 1974 after seven years of dictatorship. The last sentence of his letter to Hermkes can, therefore, be read as an expression of hope for the coming era symbolically conveyed through his reference to the timeless Greek landscape. Despo did not forget Hermkes' support and once again showed his appreciation, this time by way of a Christmas present in 1975. Despo gave Hermkes the catalogue from an exhibition about the artist Tassos presented in the National Gallery of Greece. With this present, Despo wanted to show Hermkes how the political situation in Greece during the last thirty years (ca. 1940–1974) was represented through the Arts. It appears that the gift was also meant to explain the connection between 1944 and 1974 for the people of his generation who had lived through both crucial periods. In a postcard, which was sent together with the catalogue – symbolically framing the epilogue of this era – Despo wrote: "This book is a selection of works of a left-democrat painter, who expressed in his paintings (woodcuts) what happened during the Nazi-Occupation, the civil war and the last dictatorship."[42]

Not much changed for Despo after that time. He continued travelling to Berlin for the meetings of the AdK despite his age. His return to these meetings can be also considered as practical proof of his appreciation of the Academy and its members for the selfless support they provided him during the difficult years of the dictatorship. At the same time, the example of German solidarity through this architectural network may be considered another important event among the many that prove the relationship between the two countries and their people in the field of culture as well as in both societies in general.

1 The English version of the Berlin Academy of Art's website uses the German name Akademie der Künste (AdK), a decision, which is also followed here. For more, see www.adk.de
2 An extensive body of literature exists on this topic, mainly in the Greek language. Its most recent and relevant contributions include: Dordanas Stratos, Papanastasiou Nikos (ed.), *Ο "μακρύς" Ελληνογερμανικός εικοστός αιώνας [The "long" Greek-German 20th century]* (Athens: Epikentro editions, 2018); and Evangelos Chrysos and Schultheiss Wolfgang (ed.), *Ορόσημα ελληνογερμανικών σχέσεων [Milestones of Greek-German relations]* (Athens: Foundation of the Greek Parliament, 2010).
3 For more information about the history of the AdK see: www.adk.de/en/academy
4 For more information about the AdK's building at Pariser Platz: *Akademie der Künste: Pariser Platz Berlin*, from the book-series: "Die Neuen Architekturführer," no. 69 (Berlin: Stadtwandel Verlag, 2005).
5 About the neighborhood of Hansaviertel during the Cold War era, see Jörg Haspel, Thomas Flierl (ed.), *Karl-Marx-Allee and Interbau 1957: Confrontation, competition and the co-evolution of Modernism in Berlin* (Berlin: Hendrik Bäßler, 2019); and the collective *Hansaviertel Berlin, a pocket guide to Interbau 1957* (Berlin: Bürgerverein Hansaviertel e. V., 2017). About the building and its architect Werner Düttmann, see Lisa Marei Schmidt, Kerstin Wittmann-Englert (ed.), *Werner Düttmann. Berlin. Bau. Werk.* (Berlin: Wasmuth & Zohlen, 2021).
6 www.adk.de/de/akademie, (last access 23 September 2020).
7 *Akademie der Künste 1979-1987: die Mitglieder und ihre Werke* (Berlin: Akademie der Künste, 1987).
8 For more information on Despo see Loukas Bartatilas, "Ioannis Despotopoulos (1903-1992)," in: id. (ed.), *Jan Despo: Three texts on Bauhaus* (Athens: Goethe-Institut and Benaki Museum, 2019), 22-27.
9 EPAN took its name from the combination of the two Greek words "Epistimi" (science) and "Anoikodomisi" (reconstruction). It was an interdisciplinary collective of Marxist scientists and intellectuals who dedicated themselves to the goal of the reconstruction of Greece after WW2 through their work.
10 The proposals and ideas of EPAN were mainly communicated through the magazine Ανταίος [Antaios]. All issues of Antaios were re-published together in a single volume in 2000: Ανταίος, Ελληνικό Λογοτεχνικό και Ιστορικό Αρχείο, Αθήνα 2000.
11 About the emigration wave of Greek Marxist intellectuals to Western Europe (especially to France) during the time of the Greek civil war, see Nikolas Manitakis, Servanne Jollivet (ed.), *Mataroa, 1945: From myth to history* (Athens: Asini editions, 2018).
12 Akademie der Künste [AdK], Berlin, AdK (West), Personalnachrichten Nr. 245, Bl. 26, 27.
13 Περ. "Ζυγός" [Zygos magazine], *Research for the case of the CCA*, no. 78-79 (May-June 1962), 29-47.
14 In an undated letter of Despo to the Ministry of Internal Affairs of Greece he mentions "a wish of a member, well-known philhellene, that the assembly could take place – for the first time outside Germany – in Athens, where the idea of the Academy was born, was unanimously accepted", see Archive of Ioannis Despotopoulos, Modern Greek Architecture Archives, Benaki Museum, Athens.
15 About the 1967 AdK meeting in Athens, see Loukas Bartatilas, *Architecture and politics: the role of the architect Despotopoulos to the deepening of the Greek-German relationships during the 1960s*, Online-Compendium der deutsch-griechischen Verflechtungen, https://comdeg.eu/compendium/essay/112156/ (last access 31 October 2022).
16 AdK, Berlin, AdK (West), Akademiebestand Nr. 129-10, Bl. 1–5.
17 AdK, Berlin, AdK (West), Akademiebestand Nr. 1964 Jan Despo, Bl. 36.

18 AdK, Berlin, AdK (West), Akademiebestand Nr. 129–10, Bl. 14.
19 AdK, Berlin, AdK (West), Personalnachrichten Nr. 245 Jan Despotopoulos (1964–1992), Bl. 24.
20 Ibid., Bl. 25.
21 AdK, Berlin, Hans-Scharoun-Archiv, Nr. 2836 (a), Bl. 41.
22 Many people from Despo's circle were sent to exile or chose to leave Greece.
23 AdK, Berlin, Hans-Scharoun-Archiv, Nr. 2836 (a), Bl. 41.
24 AdK, Berlin, AdK (West), Akademiebestand Nr. 222–12, Bl. 4; *Frankfurter Allgemeine Zeitung,* "Professor suspendiert" [Professor suspended], 19 October 1967.
25 AdK, Berlin, AdK (West), Akademiebestand Nr. 222–12, Bl. 1.
26 AdK, Berlin, AdK (West), Akademiebestand Nr. 222–12, Bl. 2.
27 Archive of Ioannis Despotopoulos, Modern Greek Architecture Archives, Benaki Museum, Athens.
28 AdK, Berlin, AdK (West), Akademiebestand Nr. Dok-AdK-West 335.
29 AdK, Berlin, AdK (West), Akademiebestand Nr. 129–14, Bl. 4.
30 AdK, Berlin, Bernhard-Hermkes-Archiv, Nr. 334, Bl. 60.
31 AdK, Berlin, AdK (West), Akademiebestand Nr. 2125 (2).
32 AdK, Berlin, AdK (West), Akademiebestand Nr. 129–35, Bl. 7.
33 Jan Despo, *Die ideologische Struktur der Städte,* Schriftenreihe der Akademie der Künste Nr. 4 (Berlin: Gebr. Mann Verlag, 1973).
34 AdK, Berlin, Bernhard-Hermkes-Archiv, Nr. 334, Bl. 53.
35 AdK, Berlin, Bernhard-Hermkes-Archiv, Nr. 334, Bl. 28.
36 AdK, Berlin, Bernhard-Hermkes-Archiv, Nr. 334, Bl. 25.
37 AdK, Berlin, Bernhard-Hermkes-Archiv, Nr. 334, Bl. 24.
38 Karamanlis was Greece's newly elected Prime Minister who had lived in exile in Paris between 1963–1974 where he formed a close friendship with Valery Giscard d'Estaing.
39 The KGP was illegal from the time of the civil war until the fall of the junta.
40 The dictatorship resigned right after the Turkish coup in the northern part of Cyprus in July 1974.
41 AdK, Berlin, Bernhard-Hermkes-Archiv, Nr. 334, Bl. 26. Curiously, the date on the letter is in April 1973, which is still before the end of the dictatorship. As Despo writes about facts that have already happened and we already know that these facts took place after the restoration of the Democracy and the return of Karamanlis on power, it is strongly believed that the date of April was written by mistake. The correct date of the letter can, therefore, be between August and October 1974.
42 AdK, Berlin, Bernhard-Hermkes-Archiv, Nr. 334, Bl. 19.

About the authors

Dimitrios K. Apostolopoulos (1978) is a senior researcher at the Modern Greek History Research Centre of the Academy of Athens. He holds a PhD from the history department of Technische Universität Berlin in the field of Modern and Contemporary History and conducted postdoctoral research at the University of Athens. He is the author of various publications on Greek-German postwar relations and has worked as a lecturer at several universities in Greece.

Loukas Bartatilas (1981) is an architectural historian and curator, currently completing his doctoral thesis at the Bauhaus-Universität Weimar. His research focuses on the international reception of the Bauhaus school and its impact on modern architecture in Greece through the work of the architect Ioannis Despotopoulos. He has curated the exhibition "From Building to Community: Ioannis Despotopoulos and the Bauhaus" in 2019 at the Athens Conservatory.

Frank Bösch (1969) is the director of Leibniz Centre for Contemporary History (ZZF) in Potsdam and Professor of European 20th Century History at the University of Potsdam. Previously, he was teaching at the universities of Göttingen, Bochum and Gießen. He has authored several books on the history of political parties, media history and German history in a global perspective. Currently, he is completing a book on West German relations with dictatorships worldwide since the 1950s.

Dimitris Garris (1994) is writing his doctoral dissertation on historiography and the memory of the anti-dictatorship struggle during the decades following the fall of the junta (1974–2019). His research interests include contemporary Greek and European history (19th–20th century), issues of cultural memory, the history of historiography, the history of the dictatorship 1967–1974, and the anti-dictatorship struggle, as well as the problem of trauma in history.

Vangelis Karamanolakis (1965) is Associate Professor for Theory and History of Historiography at the University of Athens (NKUA). He is also president of NKUA's historical archive and vice president of the society's board of directors of the Contemporary Social History Archives in Athens (ASKI). His recent book addresses the destruction of the files of social convictions in Greece.

Nikos Papanastasiou (1971) is Assistant Professor for Modern and Media History at the Department of Communication and Media Studies, National and Kapodistrian University of Athens (NKUA). He holds a doctorate from the University of Augsburg. His numerous publications on the interwar period and Greek-German relations in the 20th century include, for instance, "Resistance over the Radio. Pavlos Bakoyannis' clash with the Military Junta in Greece (1967–1974)" published in Greek in 2020.

Antonis Sarantidis (1988) is a PhD candidate in modern and contemporary Greek history at National and Kapodistrian University of Athens (NKUA). In 2014, he graduated from the Department of History and Archeology of National and Kapodistrian University of Athens (NKUA). His research interests focus on Greek student migration, student communities and the anti-dictatorship movement in Western Europe during the period of 1967–1974.

Hans Peter Schunk (1990) is a PhD candidate in History at the Philipps University of Marburg researching political relations of the Federal Republic of Germany with Greece, Portugal and Spain in the late 1960s and early 1970s. His research interests include historical anarchism, foreign relations of the Federal Republic of Germany, and security studies.

Chrysa Vachtsevanou (1987) is a historian specialising in post-war Greek-German relations. She holds a diploma from the Democritus University of Thrace in Komotini, Greece, and a Master's from the University of Bonn. She is currently writing her PhD thesis on Greek migration to West Germany at the University of Bonn. In addition to her doctorate, she works as a freelance editor for Deutsche Welle.

Stefan Zeppenfeld (1990) is postdoctoral researcher at the Ruhr-Universität Bochum. Previously, he conducted an oral history project at the Archive of Social Democracy of the Friedrich-Ebert-Stiftung in Bonn. He holds a PhD from the history department of the University of Potsdam. His research interests include contemporary German and European history, migration history, public history, and new approaches to everyday history.